Growing your own food

Keith Mossman

Macdonald Guidelines

Managing editor
Chester Fisher
Series editor
Jim Miles
Designer
Robert Wheeler
Picture Researcher
Linda Proud
Production
Penny Kitchenham

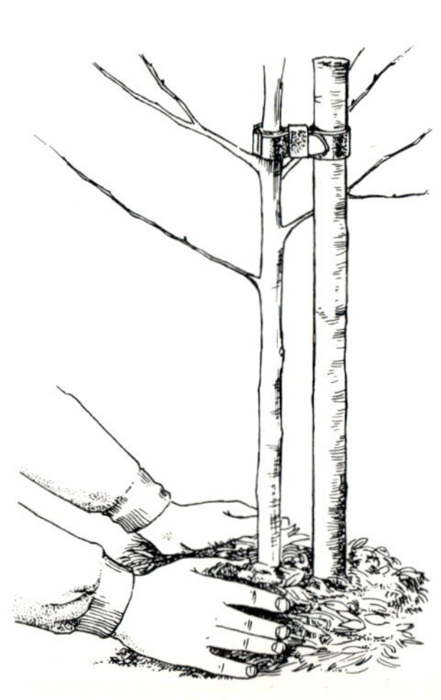

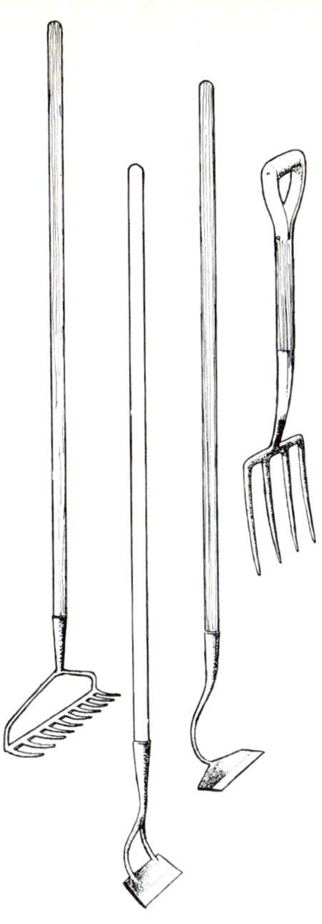

Contents

Information

Activities

Reference

First published 1978
Macdonald Educational Ltd
Holywell House
Worship Street
London EC2A 2EN
Printed and bound by
Waterlow (Dunstable) Ltd

ISBN 0 356 06023 3

Why grow your own?

An area reserved for growing vegetables and fruit was once regarded as an essential part of all but the very smallest garden. The typical cottage garden was given over almost entirely to edible crops, while in larger establishments the kitchen garden equalled the ornamental sections in importance and in its claims on time and labour.

This gradually changed. Paid professional help dwindled to a minimum and amateur gardeners 'doing their own thing' became more interested in the decorative than in the utilitarian—in looking at rather than eating the products of their efforts. The gardening press was dominated by the Garden Beautiful with hardly a glance at the Garden Useful, and seedsmen's catalogues concentrated on flowers in full colour with the vegetables which once had pride of place tucked away at the end.

The trend is now reversed, and interest in kitchen gardening is greater than for many years. The reasons are partly economic—the realization that in difficult times even the smallest garden has more than an aesthetic value. But this is by no means the whole story since the revival of home-growing for the pot, the salad bowl and the freezer was underway before the current inflation of food prices.

Quality

The quality of home-grown produce is largely a measure of its freshness. Initially, the commercially grown cabbage or lettuce may have been better than a similar article from your own plot, but by the time it reaches you, the process of distribution may have left it in a state of collapse.

Tender, leafy things are obviously nicer and less subject to waste when gathered just before being used, but there are many other aspects of freshness. The new potato transferred from soil to pot within the hour is far removed from one that has languished in dry peat for a week. The tomato picked red from the vine has the edge on the fruit gathered unripe so that it can be transported over long distances. And sweetcorn ripens after harvesting far more quickly than is realized, its sugars converting into starch and the creamy contents of the kernels into a stiff dough.

Availability

'Growing your own' also provides the opportunity to grow certain crops that are increasingly difficult to buy in a fresh, unprocessed state. This applies especially to the soft fruits, once a symbol of summer at the greengrocer's but now, with the exception of strawberries, fast disappearing. The former piles and punnets of gooseberries, blackcurrants and redcurrants, raspberries and loganberries are now sold in bulk to processors for freezing, canning or jam-making. Another vanishing fruit is the dessert plum. A perfectly ripened Victoria, let alone the luscious Cox's Golden Drop, is becoming a rarity as the acreage of commercial plums decreases and the summer markets are swamped with indifferent peaches. But a single self-fertile Victoria tree will give you fruit three years out of four.

▶ Forward planning and attention to soil requirements can enable the amateur gardener to grow a wide range of delicious home produce.

Organic gardening

Some of the recent converts to food-growing are 'organic' gardeners. They have serious reservations about modern production methods—the use of pesticides, herbicides and inorganic fertilizers. This raises a fundamental question of quality, and one sure way of knowing what you are eating is to grow it yourself. It must be recognized, however, that most gardeners do use chemical fertilizers to supplement natural plant foods.

The personal factor

Gardening is the most popular form of recreation, far more spare time being spent in the garden than in fishing or watching football, which appear to come second and third. Those to whom the garden is a relaxation and a serious hobby will find new interest in the culture of vegetables and fruit.

Work in the ornamental garden has become almost too easy; results may depend more on the amount of money spent rather than on skill. With the aid of container-grown plants, flower and shrub borders in bloom may be created overnight, but you cannot go out and buy a row of runner beans in full bearing. They must come from your own efforts, and the growing of good fruit and vegetables is indeed a real expression of gardening ability.

The money side

Just how much money you save by growing instead of buying, it is impossible to say. The total effect on the family budget will depend on the scale of operations and the value of any particular crop varies with the season or your own luck or competence. A safe assumption is that the retail value of vegetable crops will be at least three times the cost of seeds, plants, manures, fertilizers and all other current expenses.

Fruit is in a different category; there is a substantial capital outlay at the start, but little in the way of annual running costs. In bad seasons, like the droughts of 1975 and 1976, the margin over costs, based on the prices you would have to pay in the shops, is likely to be greater.

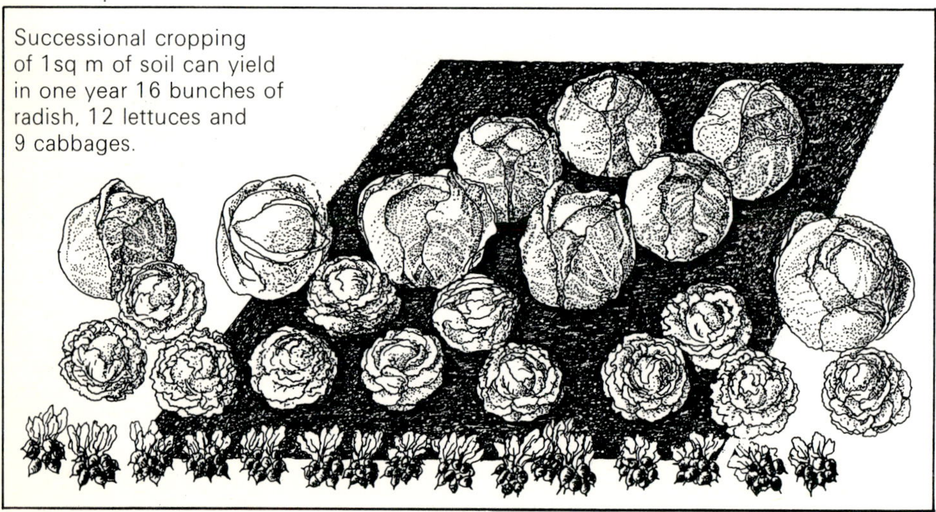

Successional cropping of 1sq m of soil can yield in one year 16 bunches of radish, 12 lettuces and 9 cabbages.

How much garden?

How much garden is needed? This question is usually asked by those considering the possibilities of food production. The upper limits to the size of your kitchen garden are determined by how much land is available and—sometimes forgotten—how much can be properly cultivated without paid help. This has to be a do-it-yourself enterprise to be financially viable. There are no lower limits; no area is so small that the attempt is not worth making.

Acquiring land

If you are already blessed with a fair-sized garden, you can expand the kitchen department by sacrificing other features. A common practice is to dig up all or part of the lawn. This has the twin virtues of simplicity and of providing ground with a reserve of fertility. As we shall see, however, there are less drastic options.

Allotments

A long decline in the area of land devoted to allotments has been followed by an upsurge in demand, so that most local authorities now have waiting lists. The first move is to ask your District Council, and, even if you get no immediate joy from them, the second move is to join the local Gardens and Allotments Society or Horticultural Society. An active society not only helps the established gardener in such matters as the bulk purchase of organic manures and the arrangement of discounts on seeds, fertilizers, and other supplies, it can be very useful to the beginner as a source of advice and information. The latter may include the future availability of allotments or other plots of land.

Time and labour

The beginner must not forget, in his enthusiasm, that the kitchen garden will not look after itself. Go cautiously when starting or expanding, so that at the end of the season you can look back with satisfaction on both the work and its results.

With the possible exception of digging, the work of the kitchen garden is no more arduous than other forms of gardening, but during the growing season, from spring to autumn, it cannot be neglected. To attempt more than can be kept under control during that crucial period ends in a disheartening mess; delayed sowings and plantings, crops swamped with weeds, and a constant struggle to catch up. Regular hoeing be-

▶ Runner beans thriving in a polythene peat-filled growing bag—a great boon to the gardener with limited space.

tween crop rows is an easy and effective method of weed control; neglect those few minutes with the hoe, and in a week or two you are faced with hours of work and a check to the crops.

The greatest return on time, effort and cash comes from the garden that is intensively cultivated, fully cropped and so planned that ground is never wasted. To achieve this aim, it is important not to take on more than you can cope with.

The very small garden

The very small, purely ornamental garden may seem to offer little scope for the growing of food crops unless one were prepared to turn the whole thing into a miniature cabbage patch—an unacceptable idea to most of us. The solution is to grow small quantities of crops which merge unobtrusively into the general scheme or are themselves intrinsically decorative. There is a wide field for experiment. Vegetables may be grown among small shrubs and herbaceous plants. Variegated kale, red-stemmed seakale beet (Ruby Chard), small clumps of sweetcorn and asparagus in rear positions and single plants of globe artichoke are examples of using crops with attractive foliage. The asparagus pea is compact and bears a mass of pink flowers, and even a patch of dwarf broad beans, though nothing to look at, can claim a scent as sweet as any in the garden.

Vertical crops

The smallest growing area usually has room for upward expansion and some crops, because of their vertical growth, give a better return than others on the soil area occupied. The runner bean is a good example, giving a very high yield for the horizontal space required. It may be grown up any kind of support and is quite ornamental, especially if red and white flowered varieties are grown together. In fact, the runner was introduced in the 18th century as a purely decorative plant and it was many years before the pods were eaten. The smaller trailing marrows and squashes may also be trained up supports and although they eventually become rather untidy, they are not unattractive when in flower. The single cordon apple or pear tree has an excellent crop-to-space ratio and requires only a 60cm width of east, south, or west-facing wall, or simple post and wire supports in open ground. Less familiar is the idea of cordon gooseberries and redcurrants on the wall, although these soft fruits were cultivated in this way in Victorian times and are now available in cordon form from many nurserymen. (Blackcurrants, unfortunately, cannot be grown as cordons.) Apart from saving space—they may be planted only 6cm apart—wall cordons are easily protected from spring frosts and bird damage to the fruit—two major problems in growing soft fruit.

Herbs and container growing

The more popular culinary herbs have a good claim on restricted space. They are widely used but not always easily obtainable in dried form. Shrubby species may be allowed to flower if trimmed back afterwards, and sage and common thyme are colourful for several weeks in mid-summer as is borage, with its blue anchusa-like blooms.

Herbs are also among the many subjects now grown in containers by those whose gardening is restricted to patio or balcony. Here one may have vegetables and salads in a variety of large containers: miniature tomatoes, such as Gardener's Delight, brightening the scene in small pots, hardy fruit trees, also in pots, and strawberries growing from the sides of barrels.

▼ A small garden can be made highly productive without turning it into an ugly vegetable patch. Make use of growing bags, attractive containers and any available wall space or fencing to cultivate a variety of plants.

Garden layout

Correct layout ensures the best possible environment for the growing crops and makes cultivation much easier. The first impulse on taking over a new, uncultivated plot, or a neglected old one, however, is to look for the easiest patch to dig and hasten to get something in. But the rectification of early mistakes causes much heart searching and upheaval which a more methodical start would prevent.

Siting vegetables

The ideal position is a completely open site exposed to the sun all day. Windbreaks, in the form of trees, are useful on the north-west to north-east perimeter, if their boughs and roots are well clear of the growing areas. On the southern side, however, obstruction to sunlight should be kept to a minimum. In mid-winter the sun is only 30° above the horizon at noon and the shadow of a tall hedge may cover the entire plot.

Siting vegetables: points to watch

Trees obscuring light

In built-up areas, one often has to manage with fairly poor light conditions and then it pays to select crops most likely to succeed in shady spots. If the vegetable plot is large and squareish in shape, it should be divided into rectangular beds by narrow working paths. This may seem to entail some loss of growing space, but in working the plot as a single bed, you eventually lose as much by making temporary paths, treading and compacting the soil. On heavy land especially, the less you tread the soil the better.

Drainage

On very badly drained land the soil of the rectangular bed may be thrown towards the centre when digging. This produces a slight camber so that water naturally drains outwards. Such a bed is drier and warmer in spring than a perfectly flat one.

Camber for adequate drainage

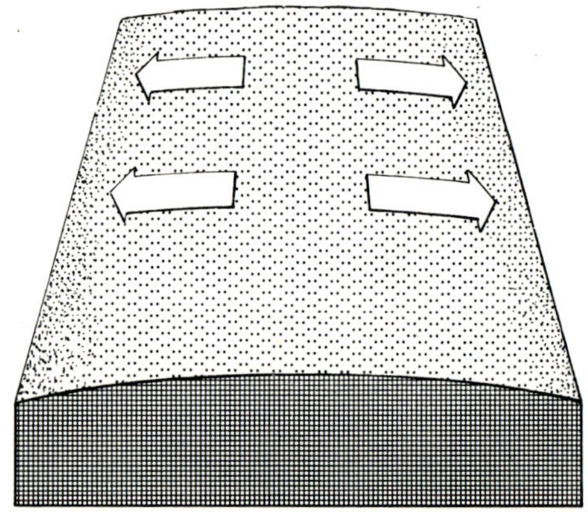

Crop rows

A north-south direction is normally best for crop rows, so that each side of the row has maximum sunlight. If the rows have to run north-south, it is wise to keep the tall crops such as runner beans, sweetcorn and Jerusalem artichokes to the northern end where their shade does not affect shorter crops. The orientation of rows is not a serious matter, but in one case there is a very definitive exception to the north-south advice; out-wintered crops under cloches do better if the rows run east-west. In this way, the low winter sun, shining mainly from the south, strikes the largest expanse of glass or plastic.

The fruit department

In the larger garden the soft fruits may be grouped together and protected in a cage, but top fruits, both trees and bushes, must usually be planted wherever the general scheme permits. Never plant fruit trees on the vegetable plot. The vegetable crops suffer from the shade and the hungry roots of the trees, and the trees may also be affected by the manures and fertilizers intended for the vegetables. Trees for the amateur gardener, especially apples, are grafted on 'dwarfing' stocks to restrict growth and produce a small, early maturing tree. Planted in a too-fertile soil, they may grow excessively despite the dwarfing effect, and be slower coming into bearing.

Fruit trees are something of a fixture and cannot easily be moved if the site first chosen fails to suit them. Avoid places where surface water collects and the soil is obviously badly drained; fruit trees cannot tolerate wet feet in winter. If the garden has a pronounced slope, plant nearer the top than the bottom. Cold air flowing downhill and spring radiation frosts so often damage the blossom. Hedges and fences to the north and east of early flowering fruits, such as currants and gooseberries, may increase yields by acting as windbreaks. Cold winds inhibit the essential pollinating insects, especially the honey bee, which always looks for blossoms in a sheltered spot.

Part of the vegetable plot may be given over to soft fruits. They may occupy the ground for up to 15 years before being replaced, so choose the site carefully. Blackcurrants may be planted closely to form a continuous hedge if you want a productive boundary between the kitchen and ornamental gardens. Gooseberries do quite well in partial shade and so do strawberries, contrary to popular belief.

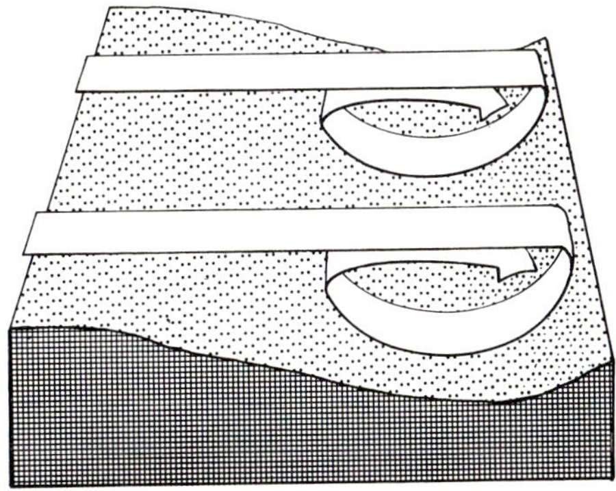
Localized frosts at the foot of sloping ground

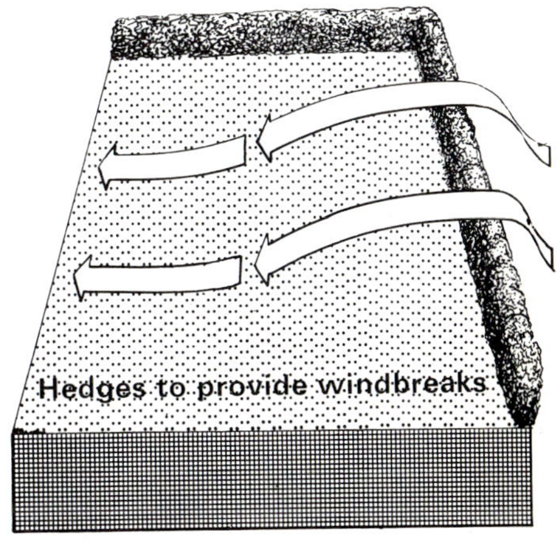
Hedges to provide windbreaks

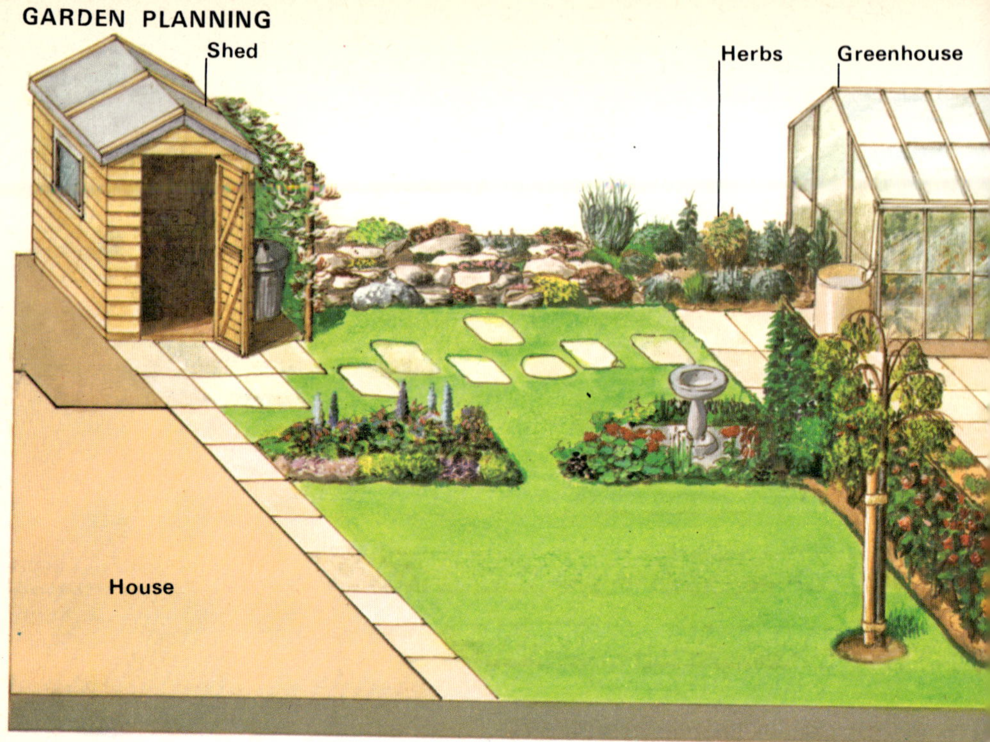

Buildings

A garden shed is usually necessary for keeping equipment and materials, storing root crops and possibly fruit, and for jobs such as potting-up. Consequently it is best sited near the house. The shed may be hidden from view by a screen if desired, and this can be put to productive use. Blackberries or loganberries, if properly supported and trained, are effective here or round the compost heap.

A greenhouse and frame should also be sited near the shed, provided the light conditions are adequate, as there is a great deal of to-ing and fro-ing between each of these at certain times during the year. It also makes sense to have the greenhouse close to the house especially if some warmth is maintained in it during the winter. Attention may be needed in bad weather and on dark evenings; temperatures have to be checked and paraffin heaters filled, and if electrical heating is installed the mains connection is usually cheaper if the household supply is close at hand.

Paths

These should give access to all cultivated areas, and the shed, greenhouse and compost heap. Make sure that all the more essential herbs can be gathered from a path. Good all-weather surfaces make for easier work. Grass, gravel or clinker is not very satisfactory so the best material is concrete. This can be laid as permanent paths but paving slabs, 60cm square and matt-surfaced, are simpler and quicker to lay.

Water supply

Although good cultivation and adequate manuring do much to maintain natural soil moisture, there always

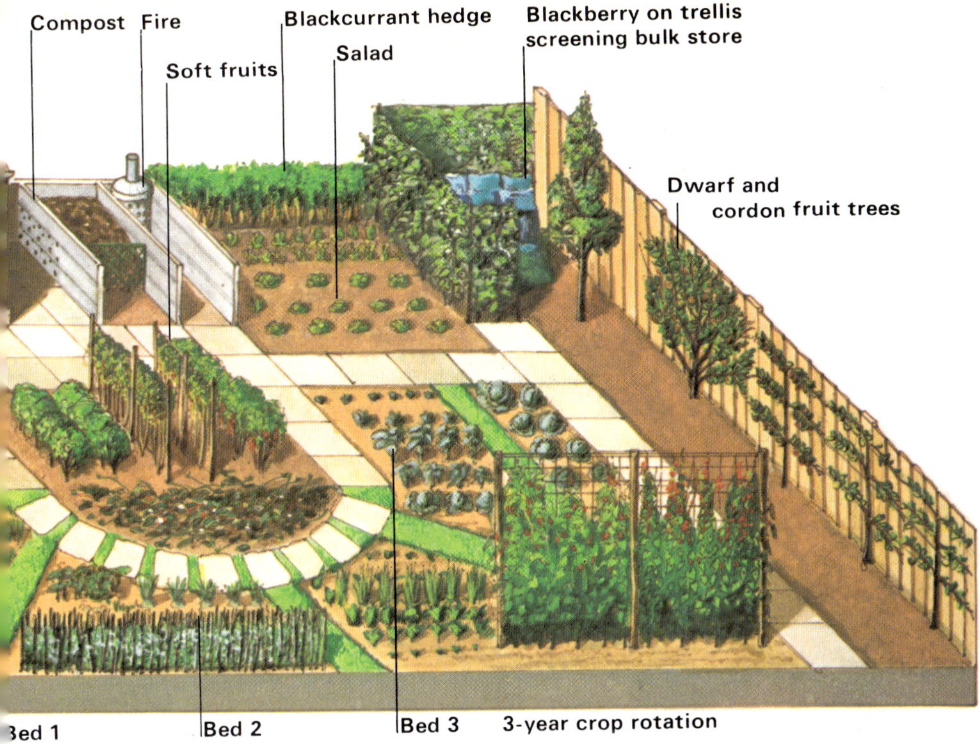

Compost
Fire
Blackcurrant hedge
Blackberry on trellis screening bulk store
Salad
Soft fruits
Dwarf and cordon fruit trees
Bed 1
Bed 2
Bed 3
3-year crop rotation

comes a time when this has to be supplemented. On a small scale, the watering can will do, as seeds and seedlings should always be watered from a can fitted with a rose, but in the larger garden a hose is almost a necessity.

runner beans
fire
compost
greenhouse
flowers
peas
salad
Bed 1
flower bed
lawn
Bed 2
blackcurrants
shed
Bed 3
House
herbs

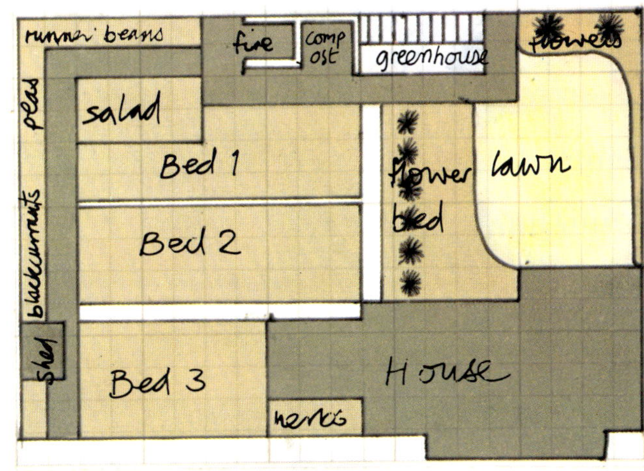

Elements in planning a productive garden
Established features: house, garage, out-buildings, north-south orientation, soil type, drainage, predominant wind. Services: shed, water supply, compost, fire, greenhouse, paving, power. Crops: 3-year rotation: beds 1, 2, 3. Fruit trees, soft fruit, climbing vegetables, herb bed, salad bed. Decorative: lawns, flower-beds, rockery, trees.

The living plant

Some understanding of plant nutrition aids good gardening. Food crops, bred to produce unnaturally large quantities of proteins and carbohydrates, must themselves be adequately fed. Plants live on inorganic materials which they collect from the earth and air, and then transform into living tissue.

Photosynthesis, food from the air

This process enables the plant to extract carbon from the air in the form of carbon dioxide. At the same time the green colouring matter of the leaves and stems (chlorophyll) absorbs the energy of sunlight providing power for the plant to build up its structure. It is often forgotten that much of a plant, from the timber of a tree trunk to the starch in a potato, comes from the air and not the soil. Deprive a plant of light and it will starve to death in the richest of soils. One group of plants, the legumes or pod-bearers like peas and beans, collects another vital element from the air. Colonies of bacteria live on the plants' roots and collect atmospheric nitrogen, to the great benefit of their hosts. These crops, therefore, need little in the way of nitrogenous manures and actually leave the soil richer in nitrogen.

Food from the soil

Three major food elements are derived from the soil. They are nitrogen, phosphorus and potassium, often referred to by their chemical symbols: N, P and K. Nitrogen promotes growth and deep green colouring in stems and leaves. Lack of it results in slow, poor growth and pale coloration. Phosphorus encourages germination and root formation. Potassium affects the whole metabolism of the plant, its resistance to disease, and the formation and ripening of seeds and fruits.

A reasonable supply of these three is

ACID AND ALKALINE SOILS
The soil's fertility is influenced by the lime content, which should be within certain limits to ensure the health of crops and of the soil itself. Lime deficiency leads to an acid or 'sour' soil; too much lime produces a very alkaline soil which may depress yields.

The acid/alkaline balance is often expressed as a 'pH' value. A reading of pH7 is neutral; above it is alkaline, and below it is acid. Most crops like a very slightly acid soil, around pH6.5. A few crops, potatoes and strawberries for instance, tolerate a more definitely acid soil, but peas, beans and the cabbage family react badly to any shortage of lime.

As a rough guide, most soils except chalky ones need a dressing of garden lime every two or three years. Chalk soils normally need no liming and even on heavy clays, where liming improves soil texture, it should not be overdone. If in doubt, a simple soil-testing kit is cheap to buy and will enable you to check the level every year.

HOW A PLANT WORKS

The leaves
In sunlight, chlorophyll, a green pigment, reacts with water brought up from the roots, and carbon dioxide, to produce the sugar which is the plant's food. Oxygen is liberated as a waste product. At night, oxygen is absorbed to break down the sugar and carbon dioxide is given off.

The stem
Conveys water and nutrients from roots to leaves. Also provides the support for the leaves and flowers.

The roots
These gather the plant's nutrients and water and anchor the plant in the soil. They serve as storage organs in some plants over the winter months.

Root hairs
They absorb the moisture and nutrients in the soil which are then conveyed to the root system proper.

vital, and in addition the plant also needs minute quantities of the so-called 'trace elements' such as magnesium. These are sometimes added to compound fertilizers, but as they exist in most average soils, we need not worry about them.

Replenishing the soil

As the nutrients in the soil are used up they have to be replaced in order that the soil's fertility is maintained. This is done naturally by decaying vegetable matter, but as the crops are removed for consumption some direct action has to be taken; only by adding compost is the natural process simulated.

Two types of plant food may be added to the soil: organics like animal manures, and inorganic chemical fertilizers. The latter come as 'straight' fertilizers, each supplying one of the three main elements, or as compounds supplying a balanced mixture of all three. Organic manures feed the soil itself, creating a long-term reservoir of fertility from which all the needs of the plants may be satisfied. The open soil texture required for a vigorous root system is also maintained. Given enough organic material, massive crops may be grown and fertility actually increased year by year as gardeners in Victorian England and the market gardeners of Paris demonstrated in the happy days of unlimited stable manure.

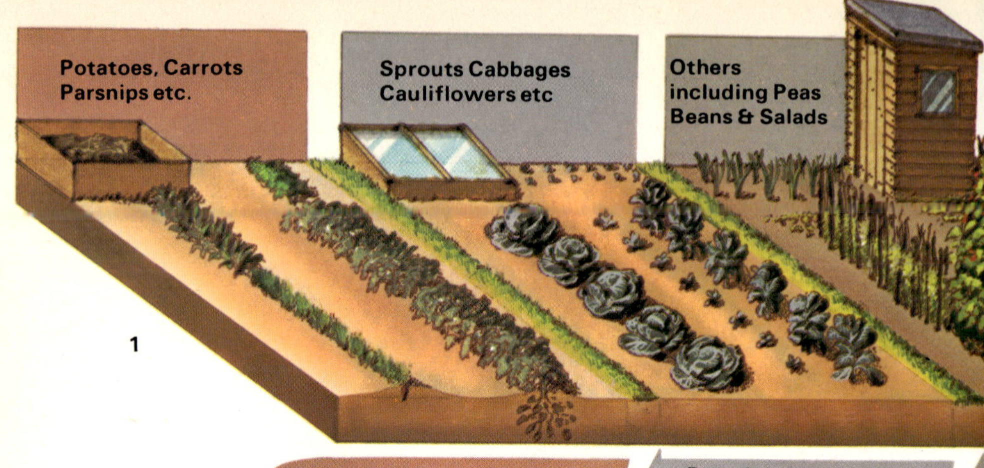

Root Crops
Fertilizer only

Brassicas
Manure and Compost
Lime (if necessary)

2

CROP ROTATION

Crop rotation is simply a method of ensuring that the same crops, or similar crops, are not grown on the same ground year after year.

There are good reasons why this should not be done. Soil-borne pests and diseases build up if their hosts are always present but fade out when they are deprived of them. This was demonstrated during World War I, when the continuous cropping of gardens and allotments with potatoes led to a disastrous outbreak of potato wart disease. In the same way the growing of brassicas without a break can result in soil infected with club root and no brassicas at all.

Again, particular crops deplete the soil of particular nutrients, and by switching crops you level up the rates of depletion. Peas and beans fix atmospheric nitrogen and enrich the soil with it Other crops would benefit from this legacy while the peas or beans would gain nothing from growing again in the same place since they could gather nitrogen anywhere.

A systematic changing round of crops also enables the best use to be made of precious supplies of organic manure. To apply it equally to all crops may be ineffective and wasteful. Some root crops for instance are

Brassicas
Manure Compost
(lime if necessary)

3

Rotation returns
to first year
scheme

generally better without fresh manure. An essential part of the rotation, therefore, is to adapt manuring to each group of crops and concentrate organic manures each year on those most likely to benefit.

In a three-year rotation the vegetable part of the kitchen is divided into three areas. Although called plots or beds for convenience, they may of course each consist of several small beds or parts of beds. Crops are divided into three groups: roots, brassicas, and a miscellaneous group comprising all other crops. Each group is, as far as possible, grown in a different one of the three areas in successive years, returning to its starting point in the fourth year. By then all crops will have made a round of the garden, which is what is meant by 'rotation'.

Organic manures are applied to the brassicas, and, to a lesser extent, to the miscellaneous group. There it is reserved for special cases like celery, cucumbers, marrows and squashes and is not dug in over the whole area.

A rotational cropping plan is a matter of commonsense and should be interpreted as a guide and not a blueprint. It can never be followed precisely, even in a large garden, and certainly not in a small one where every advantage must be taken of intercropping and successional sowings. Crops of different groups inevitably overlap, a plot starting the season devoted to one group may end it carrying a mixture of all three.

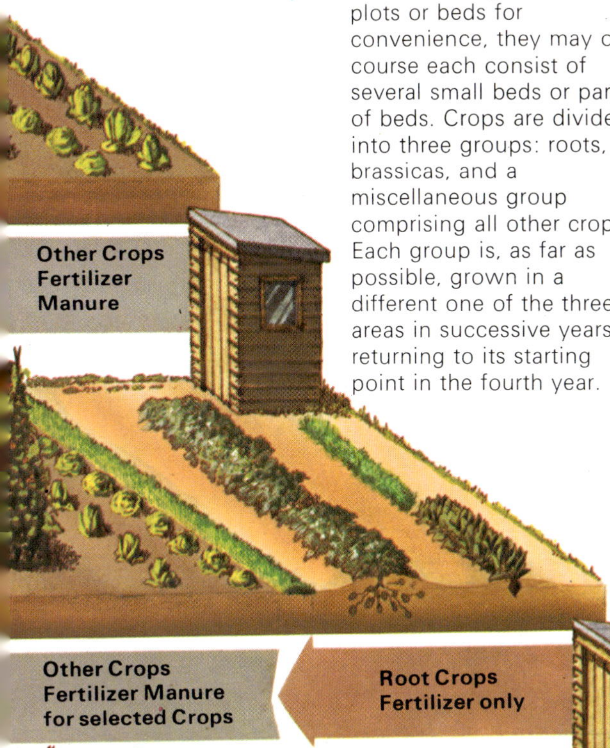

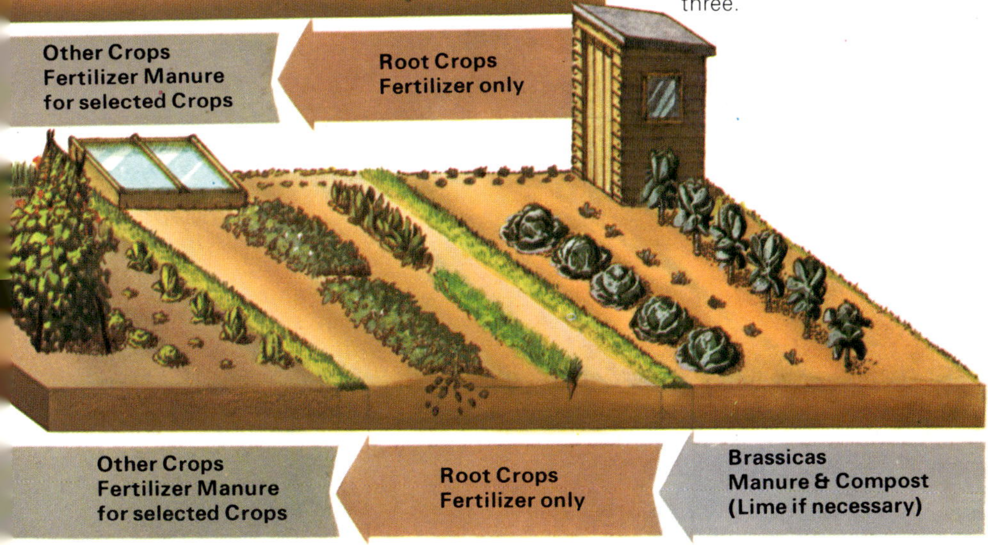

Other Crops
Fertilizer
Manure

Other Crops
Fertilizer Manure
for selected Crops

Root Crops
Fertilizer only

Other Crops
Fertilizer Manure
for selected Crops

Root Crops
Fertilizer only

Brassicas
Manure & Compost
(Lime if necessary)

Garden equipment

Buy the best tools you can afford and buy only those for which there is a clear and immediate use. Apparently 'cheap' products usually work out more expensive, not only in cash terms of breakage and replacement, but in loss of time and temper. Nor is it wise to accumulate expensive gadgetry which may or may not justify itself in the future, like, for instance, buying a flame gun for controlling weeds before testing the merits of a hoe.

THE ESSENTIAL TOOLS

The tools illustrated below are indispensable for making work easier in the average-size garden:

Digging fork and spade for primary cultivation.
Dutch hoe (1) and draw hoe (2) for surface cultivation and taking out seed drills.

Garden rake for levelling and preparing seed-beds.
Trowel and small fork for planting.
Secateurs for pruning, also pruning saw if large trees are involved.
Light wheelbarrow, garden line, watering can with coarse and fine roses, and garden hose.

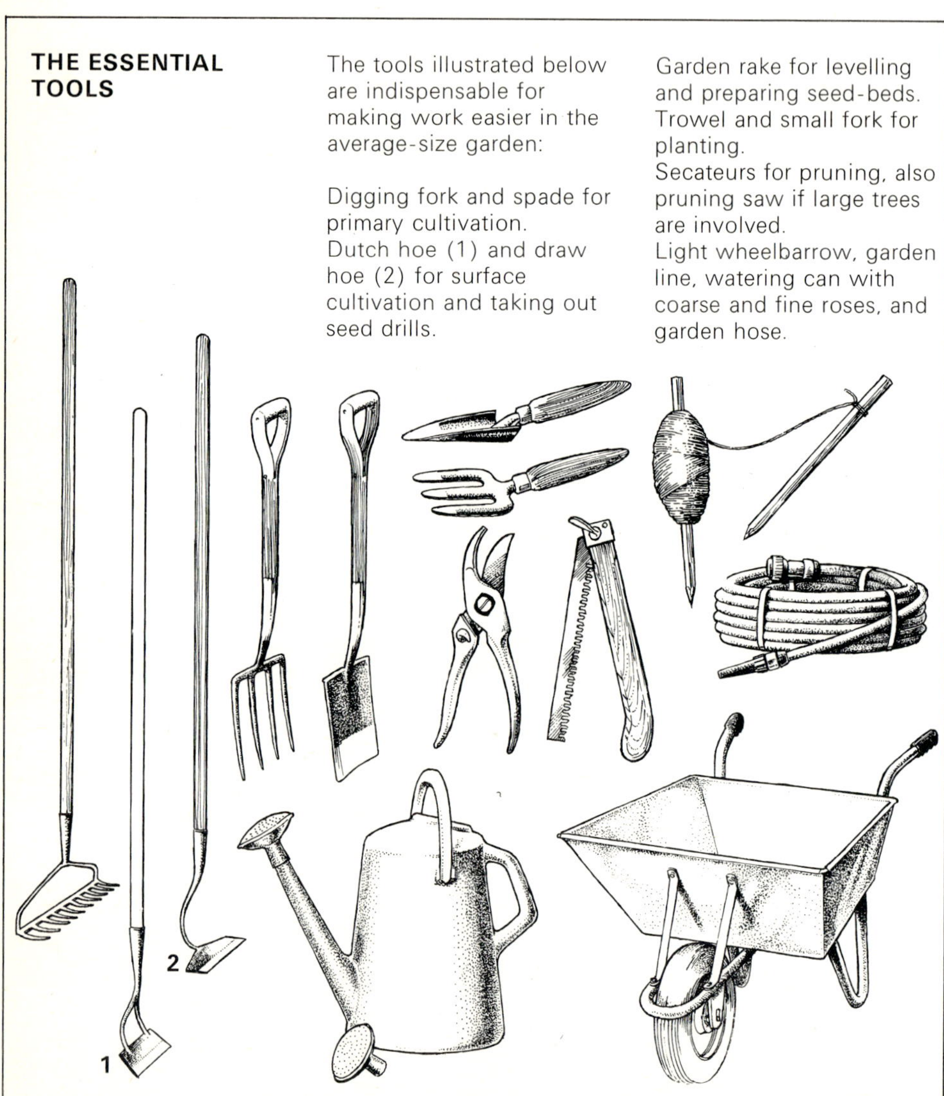

Basic tools

Choose digging tools which suit you physically. Handles are available in more than one length and spade blades in at least two sizes. On heavy land, the smaller tool is not only less tiring but may result in faster work than the standard size. Stainless steel is worth the extra cost, again for making the work easier as well as for its almost unlimited life. The best wooden handles are of ash, but non-decaying polypropylene is beginning to replace it.

The two types of hoe illustrated are used in different ways. The Dutch hoe is designed to cultivate the surface and destroy seedling weeds; you should work moving backwards leaving the hoed ground untrodden. The draw hoe serves the same purpose, though in using it you move forwards and leave the surface trodden. It is, however, a valuable tool for making all sizes and shapes of drill for seed sowing. Stainless steel hoes with metal handles and rubber or plastic grips are preferred by many gardeners and there are now many variants of the Dutch hoe.

A stainless steel trowel is a more useful planting tool than a dibber. With a pointed—not rounded—tip, it is a valuable aid when hand-weeding.

A good nylon line on a reel saves a lot of time as it is not prone to breaking at crucial moments like the usual *ad hoc* arrangement of string and sticks.

Have your garden hose fitted with a spray nozzle. Under some water authorities sprinklers are not allowed and payment of a hose rate only entitles you to use a hand-held hose.

Powered tools

The one to be seriously considered, though only for the larger garden, is the rotary cultivator or rotavator. This implement, many thousands of which are in use, consists essentially of a horizontal rotor, driven by a petrol engine, to which are attached hoe blades that chop up the soil as the machine moves forward. Depth and width of cultivation can be varied, and machines are available in many sizes.

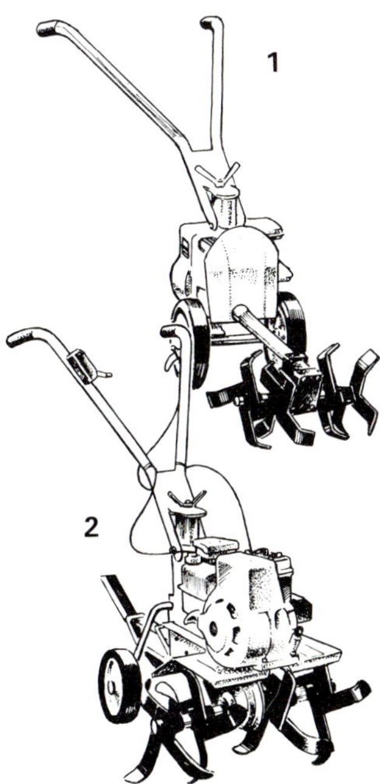

There are two types of rotavator. In one (1), the machine is pulled forward by the action of the hoe blades. The wheels are not powered and the entire thrust of the engine is concentrated on the rotor. In the other (2), the wheels are power-driven and the forward speed in relation to the speed of the rotor is regulated by gears. The slower the forward speed, the finer and deeper the tilth obtained.

As a substitute for the spade and hoe the rotavator can save a lot of time, though it has certain disadvantages, apart from cost. Modern machines, with 4-stroke engines, are very reliable, but even a small model can be tiring to operate.

Try one on hire first (see Garden Machinery Hire in the Yellow Pages telephone directory) and never buy without a demonstration of more than one model on your own ground.

The greenhouse

Output from the garden is increased by protecting crops from the weather. The tender ones have a better chance of success than they would have under outdoor conditions, and hardy crops are made available over a longer season.

Greenhouses may include plastic-covered structures. Unheated structures are known as cold greenhouses, and those with just enough heating to keep out frost as cool greenhouses.

A greenhouse has two main functions in the kitchen garden, the raising of vegetable plants such as cauliflowers, celery and marrows for later planting in the open, and the growing of tender crops such as tomatoes and cucumbers to maturity. A cold house is useful for these purposes but one providing some warmth in the early months of the year is doubly so.

Size and design are dictated by personal preference, available space, and cost. The site should be chosen for convenience of working, but it must also be as sunny as possible and well clear of trees; branches sway in high winds and greenhouses are notoriously fragile. A free-standing house should, if possible, have its longest dimension running east-west.

Greenhouse tips

Conserve sun warmth in spring by closing down all ventilation an hour before sunset.

Keep seedlings as close to the glass as possible except when sharp frost is likely.

Do not sow tender subjects for outdoor planting before mid-spring. Sown too early they become pot-bound and stunted before it is safe to plant them out.

Remember that tomatoes in pots require much more frequent watering than those grown in the border or by ring culture: up to four times a day in hot sunny weather.

Do not allow the cold house to become a mere storage dump in winter. Sow spring maturing lettuce in the borders and bring in pots of parsley. Pot-up and bring in roots of chives and mint.

▼ Four types of greenhouse: lean-to (1), bell-shaped (2), traditionally shaped (3), polythene (4).

▲ Tomatoes thriving in a traditional greenhouse. The plants must be supported either on strings or on tall canes placed in the soil.

A well laid-out greenhouse, with a solid path down the centre, makes for much easier access to the crops.

If you want to grow tomatoes or other crops in a border on the floor of the house choose a model glazed to ground level. This type is usually supplied without staging, but you can, of course, have portable staging to be removed for floor planting. If space is too tight for both a greenhouse and a garden shed, you can get a perfectly practicable combination, half shed and half lean-to greenhouse.

The main choice in construction is between timber and metal framing. Metal may be the more expensive but maintenance costs are practically nil, whereas timber must be periodically painted or treated with preservative. Since you will probably be erecting the thing yourself it should be remembered that most metal structures have simple puttyless glazing.

Greenhouse equipment

A heater is the most important item. The solid fuel, hot water system has long since vanished from the small amateur structure and the choice is between paraffin, electricity and, more rarely, gas. The blue flame paraffin heater is the cheapest to run. It requires regular cleaning and filling, although some models may be fitted with large capacity feed tanks. Plants have no objection to paraffin heaters, as they increase the carbon dioxide and moisture content of the air and this is generally beneficial, but keep the burners well maintained since smoke is harmful to plants.

For electrical heating the thermostatically controlled fan heater is recommended. It raises the temperature quickly and cuts out when the desired minimum is reached. Use only a greenhouse model with a built-in thermostat, never a household heater. Make sure that all electrical equipment is competently installed and properly earthed as there will inevitably be damp conditions.

The heater should be able to maintain a minimum temperature of 8°C in the early spring and 12°C by the end. These may seem modest objectives, but very cold nights occur over this period and are the main worry where the more tender subjects are concerned. As an alternative to heating the entire house, a heated propagator may be used for germination and the initial stages of growth. But seedlings cannot remain in it for long and as they must be grown-on in a cold house sowings cannot be made too early in the year.

The garden frame

This is simply a shallow bottomless box standing on the soil and with moveable lights for a top. Seedlings may be raised in it as in a cold greenhouse, sown either in the soil or in seed trays. In early summer it may be planted with cucumbers or melons, and in autumn with lettuce to mature in spring. It is invaluable for hardening-off plants from the greenhouse before planting out, the lights being opened for progressively longer periods and finally left off altogether.

The conventional frame light measures about 2m by 1m and slides on brick or boarded sides. Nowadays you can choose from among a great variety of designs, mostly very practical.

Site the frame with the light sloping to the south and easy access from a path, and keep sacking or other material handy for covering the glass on frosty nights. The fact that it is possible to trap the radiated soil warmth is one advantage which the frame has over the cold greenhouse.

Cloches

The original cloches, as the name suggests, were glass bell-jars, first used by French market gardeners. The modern continuous cloche, made of glass or plastic on a wire frame or of rigid moulded plastic, is so designed that any number may be used to cover an entire row or strip of several rows.

Cloches are the most adaptable form of protected cultivation. Autumn-sown lettuce, peas and broad beans are safely overwintered, and these crops, along with carrots, beetroot, dwarf and runner beans and many others, may be sown a month earlier in spring than would be practicable in open ground. Tomatoes, cucumbers, marrows, melons and sweetcorn, planted out from the greenhouse, are sheltered during their early life or in some cases right through to maturity. The height of the plant will determine whether or not you can continue to cover with cloches.

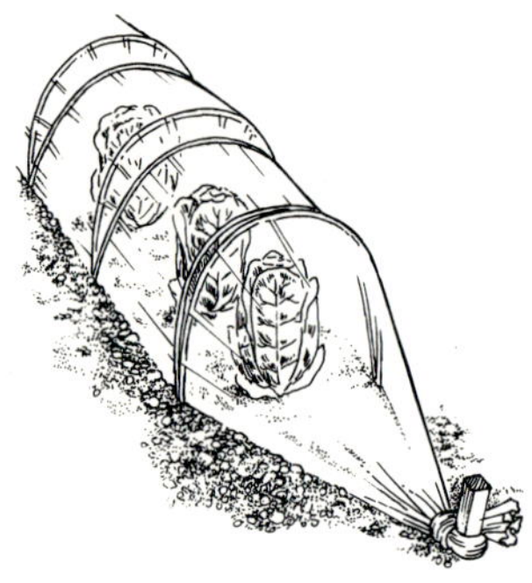

The polythene tunnel

This development of the cloche is the cheapest form of protection and is used commercially on many acres of strawberries and lettuce. Stout wire hoops are placed at intervals over the crop row, the ends being pushed well into the ground. Medium weight polythene is then stretched over the hoops and the edges buried in shallow trenches with the ends gathered together and firmly pegged down.

Preparing the soil

Soil is the basic raw material of gardening. To use it successfully you must understand its qualities and seek to remedy its defects. Soils vary greatly, but have one feature in common, division into a topsoil and a subsoil. The difference in characteristics is apparent when digging, the upper layer contains the accumulated organic material and is the fertile part, while the harder subsoil below it has not been affected by time or cultivation. Although the subsoil is relatively infertile it is very important; it affects the movement of soil moisture and the drainage of surplus water, provides certain mineral salts which are brought into the topsoil by deep-rooting plants, and largely determines the topsoil's characteristics.

TYPES OF SOIL

Soils fall into five categories, though the classification is sometimes vague. A knowledge of roughly where your soil comes in the list is nevertheless a useful guide to its treatment.

Clay soils Heavy to dig, sticky when wet, drying to intractable clods or a hard, cracked surface if wrongly handled. Impervious subsoil with poor natural drainage. Often inherently fertile, but plants tend to make poor root systems and cannot take up the available nutrients.

Dig in autumn, working in bulky organic manure to improve soil structure and leaving surface rough for frost to break down into a tilth. If liable to waterlogging, break up subsoil when digging or planting trees, but never bring it to the surface. Spring sowing and all cultivation should be carried out only when the surface is dry. Apply compound fertilizer before sowing and lime every third year unless soil tests indicate otherwise.

Good for most maincrop vegetables, but slow to warm up and therefore not so good for early crops unless cloched. Good also for fruit if not waterlogged in winter, though top fruits take time to get established.

Loam Portmanteau word for any medium soil, shading into the clays at one extreme and the sands at the other. Open and friable in texture, crumbling easily when squeezed into a ball. Easier to work than clays, often deep and fertile with plenty of humus, as in the fibrous loam of old pasture.

Maintain the soil structure by the regular application of compost or organic manures. Newly cultivated loams crop well for a time with fertilizers only, but this runs down the reserve of humus.

This is the best soil for most vegetable and fruit crops and is suitable for cloche work.

Light or sandy soil Easily worked, free-draining, usually overlying gravelly subsoil. Typically a 'hungry' soil, needing bulky manures to retain moisture, and fertilizers to replace the chemical elements leached out by rain. Plants make very large root systems searching for moisture and food and so are able to respond to top dressing and liquid feeding.

Apply manure or compost during winter digging and compound fertilizer before sowing or planting. Water in dry weather and mulch with peat or rotted manure, especially in the case of raspberries, blackcurrants and wall fruit. Suspect lime or potash deficiency if crops fail or fruit trees or bushes show poor growth.

Good for early and overwintered crops in the open and for the earliest cloche crops. Also for long varieties of root crops which fail on clays.

Chalk soil Alkaline, sometimes greyish in colour, with

a chalk or limestone subsoil. Drains and dries out fast but apt to be sticky immediately after rain. Probably never needs liming but naturally deficient in plant foods, especially nitrogen.

Organic manures break down quickly in alkaline soils, which need all they can get. Peat may be used in unlimited quantities without fear of creating acid conditions. Use a compound fertilizer for pre-sowing application and top dress with a nitrogenous fertilizer if a crop is stunted or yellowing.

Good for peas, beans, brassicas and stone fruit, such as plums. Soft fruit should be mulched annually with peat or rotted manure. Potatoes, often affected in yield and quality by the high pH, should be planted in peat-lined trenches.

Peat soils There are two types, fen soils and acid moorland peats. The first are deep, very fertile and not noticeably acid. They are formed in rivers carrying dissolved mineral salts, and are full of plant nutrients. Moorland peats are formed by the accumulation of decaying vegetable matter in stagnant water and are badly drained and very acid.

Fen soils do not create any problems but few gardeners are lucky enough to have them. Acid peats need drainage, lime and fertilizers, but not organic manures. The range of crops will depend on the degree of acidity. One that does well in such soils, and practically nowhere else, is the blueberry.

Digging

Whatever the soil, digging is the first act of cultivation. Digging enables the compacted topsoil to be broken up and air and water to enter the soil. It also breaks up the subsoil where required, thus improving drainage and the upward movement of soil moisture in dry weather. Digging is also necessary to mix in bulky manures and to remove or bury annual weeds and remove the roots of perennial weeds.

When to dig

Dig all vacant ground in autumn or early winter, leaving the surface lumpy. Water in the clods freezes, expands and shatters them from within, so that when dry in spring they break down into a fine tilth. The ground should be dry or lightly frozen—no harm is done by turning in a few centimetres or so of frozen soil.

Digging heavy land in summer, prior to sowing crops in succession, presents problems when you want to get a tilth. It is best to avoid digging and rely on surface cultivation with the hoe. Otherwise, dig in dry, sunny weather, break the soil into small lumps and allow them to dry out completely. Then use a hose to soak thoroughly and the following day the lumps can be raked into a tilth.

How to dig

Use a spade rather than a fork unless the soil is too sticky. Start at a corner of the plot. Place a foot on a shoulder of the blade and drive it vertically into the ground with the weight of the body. Pull the handle back to lever up the piece of soil, slide one hand down the shaft to the point of balance, lift and throw the soil forwards, inverting the blade so that it slips off.

Work across to the far boundary, keeping a straight

▼ Plain digging.

▼ An alternative to double digging.

trench with a vertical face. If you insert the spade at an angle the work will be shallower and less tidy and some of the topsoil will not be moved.

On reaching the far side, scrape the spade clean with a trowel or a piece of wood, walk back to the beginning and start again. Maintain a leisurely rhythm and dig only a narrow strip each time so that you do not have to lift large and heavy clods.

Digging one spit deep in this way is known as plain digging. Trenching, or double digging, in which the subsoil also is dug, is a more elaborate operation for which few now seem to have the time or energy. A simpler alternative is possible if you want to improve a hard subsoil which is impeding drainage. Complete a row of plain digging with the spade, leaving a clearly defined trench. Then take the fork and break up the subsoil along the floor of the trench. Do not attempt to lift and turn the subsoil, simply drive the fork in and lever it up all along the trench so that it is left broken and fissured. Repeat with each row of digging. The effects in better drainage and root penetration on heavy clays are worth the modest extra effort.

When digging in manure or compost, take it from the barrow or strategically placed heaps; do not spread it over the undug surface. And distribute it up the far side of the trench so that it is thoroughly mixed with the soil and not left in a separate layer between topsoil and subsoil.

When digging up grass for the first time, the most satisfactory method is to pare-off the turf with the spade to a depth of 4cm, stacking it grass down in a neat pile which will moulder into good potting soil. Then dig in the usual way, removing large perennial weed roots. Alternatively, you could apply sodium chlorate, which would kill even perennial weeds but would leave the ground unsafe for planting until rain had washed it out—at least six months from an autumn application and a year from a spring one.

▼ Digging in compost or manure.

Manure

No matter how good your soil is initially, it must receive some organic material to maintain fertility.

Farmyard and stable manure Rare commodities in urban areas. Stable manure is obtainable from riding stables, farmyard manure when cattle yards are cleared in early summer.

Dried poultry manure A rich source of nitrogen. Obtainable from garden shops or direct from some poultry farms.

Spent mushroom compost One of the best soil foods on the market. But it is high in chalk content and so is unsuitable for potatoes. Look up Mushroom Growers in the Yellow Pages telephone directory, as many sell this to gardeners.

Spent hops Small independent breweries (Yellow Pages again) sometimes give small quantities away. Otherwise it is dried and sold as hop manure.

Processed organics Dried blood, fish-meal, bonemeal, hoof and horn. Valuable but expensive substitutes for inorganic fertilizers used by those with strong

▼ Green manuring.

objections to the latter. Dried blood and fish-meal are strongly nitrogenous, hoof and horn releases nitrogen slowly over a long period and bone-meal does the same with phosphates. None has enough bulk to improve soil structure.

Peat Although not an immediate source of plant food, peat is a useful soil conditioner increasing the humus content and opening up heavy soils. On sandy or chalk soils, either dug in or used as a mulch, it may be used freely.

Green manuring This is a very old method of building up humus in poor, light soils which should be more widely used. In late summer hoe and rake any vacant pieces of ground to obtain a tilth. Scatter over it about 30g per sq m of sulphate of ammonia and 30g per sq m of mustard seed. Rake in and in dry weather keep watered until germination in about four days. When the mustard is 25 to 30cm high dig it in, turning the spit over and making sure that all the greenery is buried.

Making compost

Garden compost is the cheapest manure. There is nothing mysterious about it, the process is merely a way of returning vegetable waste to the soil in the most convenient and—from a plant's viewpoint—useful form.

Compost can be made in containers for the sake of tidiness but is equally good made in heaps. A heap for an average garden should take up about 2 sq m although there should be room for two heaps. Keep free of perennial weeds and never make compost on a concrete or other solid base which impedes drainage and prevents the entry of earthworms.

At one end of the site accumulate a layer of garden waste 30cm deep. Sprinkle it lightly with sulphate of ammonia or a proprietary activator. Water it well and cover with 3cm of soil. Build up a second layer of waste, sprinkle it with a handful of garden lime, then water, cover with soil and repeat the sequence until the heap is about 1m high. Leave it for a couple of months, then turn it onto the adjoining space, placing uncomposted stuff from the outside in the centre of the heap. Cover with soil, and, in persistently wet weather, with polythene sheeting. The compost is ready for use when brown and crumbly.

If small quantities of manure from pigeons, rabbits or backyard poultry are available use it in the heap instead of the chemical activator in 5cm layers.

Suitable matter Annual weeds and the tops, but not the roots, of perennial weeds. Crop residues, pea and bean vines, brassica leaves, tops of root crops. Discarded bedding plants, lawn mowings, soft, but not woody, hedge trimmings. Household waste fruit and vegetable peelings and trimmings, tea and coffee grounds, dead flowers, but not edible scraps like bread crusts which attract vermin.

Fertilizers

Chemical fertilizers supply the main food elements im-

The compost heap

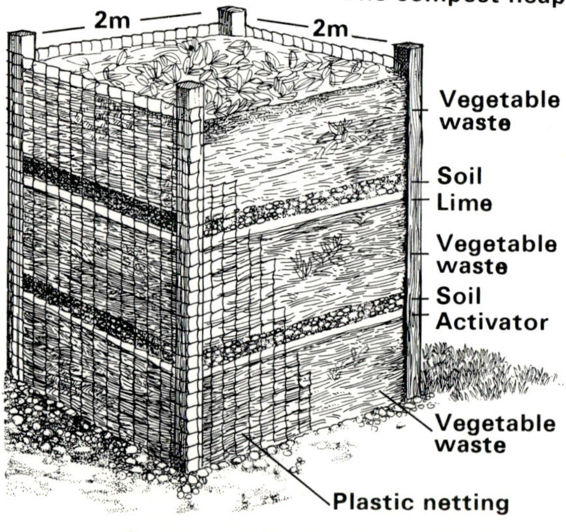

mediately and in concentrated form. They are applied close to the surface, are easily soluble so roots can take them up, and are no use unless the soil is moist. They are also soon washed out of the soil with little or no carry-over from year to year. The following are used to provide specific elements.

Nitrogen Sulphate of ammonia. Apply at 30g per sq m before sowing or 15g per 1m of row as a top dressing. Nitro chalk, use on acid soils at the same rates. Nitrate of soda, expensive, quick acting, apply as top dressing at 15g per 1m of row.

Phosphorus Commonly referred to as phosphates. Most used is superphosphate of lime, applied at 45 to 60g per sq m before sowing or planting.

Potassium Commonly referred to as potash. Sulphate of potash is the one to use, applied at the rate of 30g per sq m. Not often necessary as a straight fertilizer, though sometimes advised on light soils. Many fruits, especially gooseberries, are intolerant of potash deficiency.

Compound or general fertilizers These are balanced mixtures of the above chemical foods and the most useful for the amateur. Usually applied before sowing at 60 to 90g per sq m. The National Growmore formulation is a typical and very reliable one.

Lime Ground limestone, ground chalk, or hydrated lime. Never use quicklime. Apply 180 to 240g per sq m after digging.

Solid fertilizers Store under dry conditions and, if possible, buy only enough to last the current season. Fertilizers absorb moisture and easily degenerate into a squashy mess. You can estimate the dose accurately enough by weighing a given number of handfuls and working out the weight per handful.

When applying a pre-sowing dressing, scatter the fertilizer evenly a week before the sowing date and lightly fork or rake it in. There are a few exceptions to this, as in the case of potatoes, where the fertilizer may be scattered along the planting trench round the tubers.

In top dressing, distribute the fertilizer evenly alongside the row, hoe it in very lightly, and, if the weather and soil are dry, water thoroughly. Keep the fertilizer off the foliage and never exceed the maximum dose advised.

▼ Liquid fertilizers should not be poured over the foliage of seedlings—apply to the base of the plants.

Liquid fertilizers
Here the chemicals are already in solution, and when diluted to the proper strength are very quickly taken up by the plants. Although used mostly in the greenhouse, they are valuable for outdoor crops which seem to be lagging. Do not try to give an extra boost by using a stronger dilution than that recommended by the makers; feed more often if the crop appears to need it. At the proper strength the liquid is harmless to most foliage but should not be poured over the leaves of young seedlings. Very dry soil should be watered before application.

Foliar feeds
In this new technique, liquid feeds are sprayed on to the foliage and appear to be absorbed into the plant's tissues in a matter of hours compared with days or weeks when taken up from the soil.

Although proving its value on many glasshouse crops, foliar feeding is not generally accepted for garden use. It is worth a trial, treating one half of several crop rows and leaving the untreated halves as controls.

Foliar feeds are obtainable in small quantities from garden shops. Ordinary liquid fertilizers must *not* be used in this way.

Seeds and sowing

Next to the soil, the gardener's most important raw materials are the seeds and plants he entrusts to it. Upon their potentiality for growth and yield depends the final result.

The seed and nursery trades maintain a high standard for their products, and crop failure is seldom their responsibility. Usually it follows poor cultivation or bad luck, but newcomers to gardening also come unstuck through choosing wrong varieties, and care in the selection of vegetable seeds and plants and fruit trees and bushes is essential.

The seed catalogue

Get your name on the mailing list of one or more of the large seedsmen, even if you intend to buy some seeds locally. Their catalogues offer the widest choice, much general information, and the latest on new varieties.

Work out a rough cropping plan for the season based on your priorities for the various crops, the space available, and using the table of planting distances on pages 62–67. It is impossible to give general guidance on how much seed to buy because few varieties are now sold by weight and packet contents and prices vary. But catalogues usually specify the length of row or number of plants to be expected from each packet and this serves as a useful guide.

Remember that the order should include seeds for sowings later in the season, for successional crops of carrots, turnips and beet, for perpetual spinach, spring cabbage and winter lettuce sown from mid-summer onwards.

Choice of varieties

In a new district, or when first making a start, seek the advice of gardening neighbours. Study the catalogues and note the names of cultivars which appear in all of them—the old reliables. Be wary of sensational novelties and let others try them out first. This does not mean that you should shun all new introductions—rather that you should test just one or two every year and compare their performance with that of established favourites.

You will notice that an increasing number of varieties are described as F_1 hybrids and are more expensive than non-hybrid varieties. They are characterized by increased vigour and yields and are likely to be the most valuable of the novelties.

Some varieties will prove better adapted than others to your particular soil and climate. On heavy clays and shallow chalk lands, for example, grow stump-rooted carrots and parsnips rather than long ones. On a dry, sandy soil where ordinary summer spinach runs to seed instead of leaf, try the New Zealand variety, or perpetual spinach. In a cold, exposed district where runner beans suffer badly from high winds, rely on dwarf French beans or the dwarf runner, Hammonds Dwarf Scarlet.

Pelleted seeds

Many varieties of small seeds are now sold covered with a protective coating. The smallest seeds are thus made large enough to be individually placed, resulting in thinner and more regular sowing. Handle and store pelleted seeds with care to ensure that the protective material is not broken.

Storing and saving seeds

Seeds should be stored in completely dry conditions at normal room temperatures. They are not harmed by cold, but dampness is fatal. The viability of seeds varies greatly between species and the list of storage times we give is only a rough guide. (See pages 62–67).

The storage of 'seed' potatoes and onion sets prior to planting is a differ-

ent matter; they are already on the verge of active growth. Pack the potatoes closely in shallow boxes, ends with the most eyes uppermost, and keep them in full light but safe from frost. Here they will develop stout green shoots to give them a good start.

Onion sets, too, should be removed from bags before acquiring long white shoots. Spread them out in a cool, light place.

Small seeds from your own crops are rarely worth saving, though peas and beans too old for culinary use may be left on the vine until the pods are dry, then shelled and, after a few more days drying, stored in envelopes bearing the names of the varieties. If this is done for one year only, you need not worry about selecting large, well-shaped pods, as the seeds of all except F_1 hybrids will carry the genetic make-up of the parent whatever the quality of the pods. But naturally if you continued saving seed from plants producing a number of inferior pods the strain would deteriorate.

Never save the seed of F_1 hybrids. They are bred by crossing two distinct parent lines and cannot reproduce their own characteristics. Seeds of brassica plants should also not be saved. Cross-fertilization occurs easily among members of the cabbage family and the resultant progeny may be peculiar and unprofitable.

▲ Seedlings pushing their way up through the soil.

Sowing and potting composts

Plants grown in the restricted conditions of boxes and pots, with their limited root-run, require special soils, free from insect pests and disease spores and well supplied with nutrients. Although these soils are called 'composts' they are quite different to the garden compost used as manure.

Most gardeners buy ready-mixed composts, either of the John Innes or loam-based type, or soil-less products based on peat.

The John Innes (JI) range consists of seed compost and three potting composts, JI 1, 2 and 3. All consist of sterilized loam, coarse sand and peat, with a specially formulated fertilizer called John Innes Base. The potting composts differ only in the amount of JI base they contain, JI 3, for instance, containing the most, and being most suitable for large plants in large containers. The JI composts are excellent for tomatoes and other under-glass crops. But the composts vary with the quality of the loam.

Soil-less composts like Levington are standardized products, uniform in composition and performance. They are light, clean to handle and encourage rapid growth with plenty of root. Consisting largely of peat, they should be kept damp. If the compost does get dry it should be spread out, sprinkled with warm water from a rosed can, stirred well and repacked tightly in the bag.

The drying out of soil-less compost in which plants are growing is indicated by the surface becoming pale in colour and the container a lot lighter in weight. If this happens to small seedlings, place them in the shade and water them lightly and repeatedly through a fine rose. It is useless to apply a lot of water until the peat is able to absorb it. A dried-out pot plant is best re-wetted by immersing the pot in water until air bubbles cease to rise from the compost.

Containers

Small seeds are sown in seed trays or pans and later pricked out into larger trays or singly into small pots. Larger seeds may be sown directly into pots. Plastic trays are preferable to wooden seed boxes; they last longer, are easily cleaned and do not harbour spores of fungus diseases. Plastic pots are lighter and less breakable than clays, which they are now generally replacing.

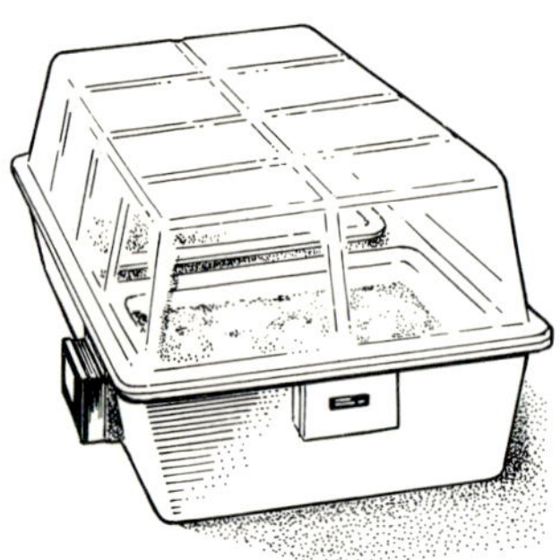

▲ The electric propagator is a fairly certain way of ensuring seed germination.

Peat pots are worth their slight extra cost when raising the more valuable crops for planting out. The pot, made of compressed peat, is itself planted; the roots of its occupant penetrate the sides as the peat softens underground, and the plant establishes itself without a check. The extra cost is, of course, due to the fact that the pot can only be used once.

A possible alternative to any sort of pot is the Jiffy 7, a thick disc of highly compressed peat and plant foods enclosed in fine-mesh net. It is about 2cm in diameter and when soaked in water expands into a 5cm high column of soil in which seeds may be sown or a cutting inserted. Jiffy 7s are useful for those gardening in cramped quarters like the kitchen windowsill. They enable the equivalent of many small pots ready filled with compost to be stored in a small box.

Sowing small seeds

Fill the seed tray with compost, firm it with light pressure, leaving a level surface

▲ Sieve soil to achieve a fine tilth.

at least 1cm below the rim. Sow the seed thinly, cover quite lightly with compost, and water gently from a fine rose. Cover with a sheet of glass and a piece of cardboard, or with black polythene to retain moisture. Inspect daily, remove the covering at the first sign of germination, and keep the seedlings in full light.

If pelleted seed is used, the pellets may be spaced 4–5cm apart making pricking out unnecessary if the tray is deep enough for the development of sturdy plants. Non-pelleted seeds produce more crowded seedlings which must be given room for development by pricking out into trays or pots of potting compost. Do this as early as possible, preferably before the seedlings form their first true leaves. Lift each seedling with a small pointed seed label or a penknife, holding it by a seed leaf rather than by the stem, which is easily crushed. Make a hole in the potting compost deep enough to insert the seedling almost up to the seed leaves, and gently firm the compost round it after planting. Pricking out is easier when soil-less compost is used. It clings to the rootlets when the seedling is lifted and the little plant quickly re-establishes itself.

▲ Pricking out young seedlings.

Sowing large seeds

Seeds of marrows, cucumbers, melons, and sweetcorn are large enough to be sown individually in pots, avoiding pricking out. Relatively few plants of these crops are needed, and as they are all tender varieties they should not be sown until at least a month after the hardies such as summer cauliflowers and cabbages, even in a greenhouse with some heat.

Fill the required number of 6–7cm peat pots with potting, not seed, compost. Firm it so that it is well below the pot rim. Sow two or three seeds in each pot and on germination reduce the seedlings to the one strongest in each pot. In sowing, simply push the seeds 1cm deep into the compost, water, and cover the pots until germination. Seeds of marrows, squashes, courgettes, cucumbers and melons should be pushed in edgeways, not flat.

Keep in the warmest part of the greenhouse until germination, then continue growing close to the glass.

Sowing outdoors

Conditions for germination are moisture, air and a certain degree of warmth. Soil must be moist but not waterlogged, and spring sowing must not start until the soil has had time to warm up.

The top 2cm or so of soil should be fine and friable, the condition described as 'a good tilth'. This is more important for the smaller seeds—peas and beans produce larger and tougher shoots than, say, onion seeds, and can push their way up through a more knobbly covering—but all seedlings must be able to send their rootlets down and expand their first leaves to the light without serious obstruction if they are to survive.

Winter digging and exposure of the surface to frost are the best ways of ensuring a tilth. When the soil is dry enough to work, lighter in colour and no longer sticking to the boots, you can, if soil and air temperatures are reasonable, begin operations.

Correct sowing dates in the early months of the year are not simply a question of reference to the calendar. They vary from season to season, from district to district, and with the hardiness of the crop. Recommended dates are meant only as general guidance, to be interpreted in the light of local weather and soil conditions. The general state of vegetation is a surer guide than the date; when grass and weeds show signs of growth, and early daffodils are opening, you may start sowing the hardier crops.

The seed bed

This can mean (a) any ground prepared for sowing and (b) a small plot earmarked for the raising of plants such as cabbages for later transplanting. Here we are concerned with the first.

Rake the surface level when the soil is dry enough to work, removing large stones and any clods which refuse to break down. Apply fertilizer at this stage, raking it well in. It is advisable to allow about one week between fertilizer application and sowing, and as the surface will now be sticky with wetter soil brought up by the raking, you should give it time to dry again before starting to sow.

▼ Raking to a fine tilth.

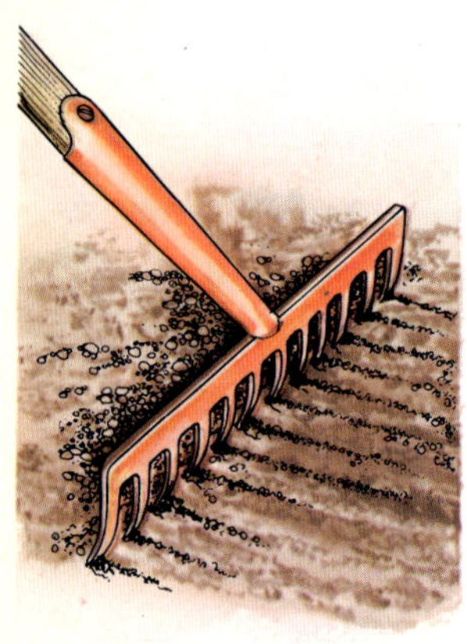

▼ Making a drill with edge of hoe blade.

Decide on the spacing between rows before starting operations. Don't overcrowd.

Always use a line to ensure straight rows. Make sure the line is taut, then take out a drill with the draw hoe, walking backwards and keeping the hoe blade in contact with the line.

The drill for small seeds is V-shaped and made with a corner of the hoe blade. That for larger seeds like peas and beans is made with the full width of the blade and is a shallow flat-bottomed trench. The correct depth varies somewhat with the size of the seed, the time of year and the state of the soil.

▲ Release seeds between thumb and forefinger.

Small seeds such as carrots, turnips and lettuce are in theory better if only just covered, though in practice they must have enough cover to keep them moist when the surface dries. Again, the soil in spring is warmer just below the surface than at deeper levels, a further reason for shallow sowing. In late spring and

▼ Firming down soil over the seeds.

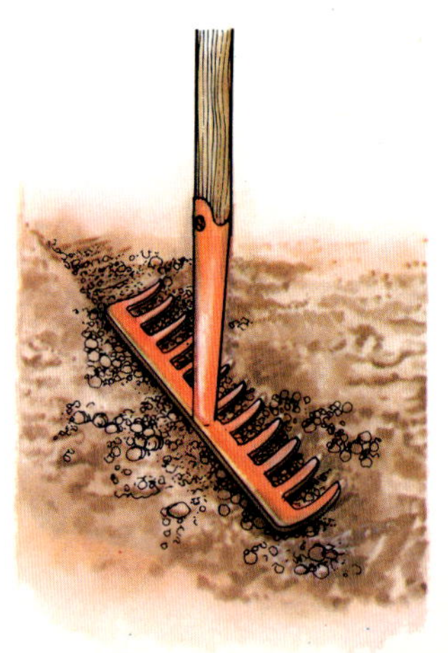

summer the soil is warm enough for germination to a considerable depth, and the conservation of moisture is more of a problem, so later sowings may be a little deeper than early ones. In general, though, more sowings are lost from being too deep than from being too near the surface.

To sow small seed, empty a little from the packet into the palm of the hand and release it slowly between thumb and forefinger, moving along the drill. Keep the hand close to the soil, especially in windy weather and when sowing light, bulky seeds like parsnip. Sow as evenly as possible but not too sparsely. Beans are individually spaced in a staggered double row in the wide drill, and though the operation may seem tedious, peas also benefit from individual sowing and should be placed about 2cm apart.

▲ Thinning out seedlings.

▼ Protect from birds with cotton (below) or nylon netting.

The sowing of pelleted seed has its own problems. The pellets are large enough to be handled separately, so that the seedlings are spaced far enough apart to facilitate the work of thinning.

But you cannot, as sometimes suggested, sow the pellets at the final spacing of the drop. That is to say, if you want a row of carrots to stand eventually at 10cm apart, you cannot sow one pelleted carrot seed every 10cm and expect to get a full crop. Casualties are inevitable, and a safe rule with pellets is to sow them not more than 2cm apart and thin as necessary. The warning against sowing too deeply applies especially to pelleted seeds. Ideally, they should be only just covered, but at the same time they *must* be kept moist, which in dry weather can mean daily watering until germination. Having sown one row, cover the seed by drawing the soil back over the drill with the hoe or the back of the rake and lightly firming it with the flat of the hoe blade.

Successional sowings

Quick maturing crops sown after the clearance of main crops are a feature of the productive garden.

Clear away the old crop without delay, cultivate lightly with fork, hoe or rotavator, but avoid deep digging, which at this time of year causes serious loss of moisture. In dry weather, soak the bottom of the drill thoroughly before sowing. Continued watering may be necessary until the seedlings are established, and it must be remembered that a germinating seed once allowed to dry out, is finished for good.

Causes of failure

Failure to germinate is rarely due to the quality of seed. It may be attributable to the soil being too cold or too dry, but often the non-appearance of a sowing is a failure of emergence rather than of germination.

If all or most of a sowing fails it may be possible to diagnose the reason by digging up a few seeds, though only the larger ones can usually be found. If the seed is hard and unaltered, the soil is too dry. If soft and rotten, it is waterlogged or too cold. If the shoot or rootlet has been eaten off, the culprits are probably leather jackets, wireworms or small slugs, and an appropriate pesticide should be used before re-sowing. If the shoot has been nipped off just below the surface, birds are most likely to blame.

Plants and planting

'Plants' includes vegetables and salad plants, fruit trees and bushes. The common feature of these particular crops is that at some stage they are transplanted, unlike crops which mature where they are sown. A major difference is that vegetables are moved when in active growth, whereas fruits, with the exception of strawberries, are transplanted when dormant.

VEGETABLES

Buying plants

Crops most likely to be bought in as plants are the brassicas, leeks, celery, and the tender species like tomatoes which you may not have the facilities to raise from seed.

Grow your own plants where possible; they usually suffer less in transplanting than bought ones. Equally important is the fact that your choice of varieties will be as wide as the seed catalogue, whereas the nurseryman will probably be able to offer you only a limited range of the most popular cultivars. About 80 per cent of tomato plants sold are Moneymaker, a reliable but unexciting variety.

If you want a yellow-fruited tomato, a large sweet Continental type like Big Boy or a miniature, or even an old-established dwarf bush variety such as The Amateur, the chances are that you will have to grow it yourself.

The best way of buying plants is to contact a local nurseryman early in the season, order the plants and find out when they will be available. The worst way is to buy on impulse from a chain store plants that have been too long out of the ground or have been left for days without water in pots or boxes. Go for sturdy, short-jointed, deep green specimens with the spreading leaves that indicate plenty of room in infancy. Avoid like the plague the lean and leggy cabbage, and the purplish-leaved tomato forced into premature bloom by starvation.

Planting

Transplanting is something of a surgical operation, and the aim must be to reduce shock and enable the plant to resume its interrupted growth as quickly as possible.

Hardy crops Prepare the planting site in good time to allow the soil to settle after digging, and rake in a pre-planting dose of fertilizer if required. If the plants are coming from your own seed-bed water them thoroughly several hours before lifting in dry weather. Lift carefully with trowel or small hand fork, keeping the soil round the roots of each plant. Never pull them up, and don't leave them lying about for hours before planting.

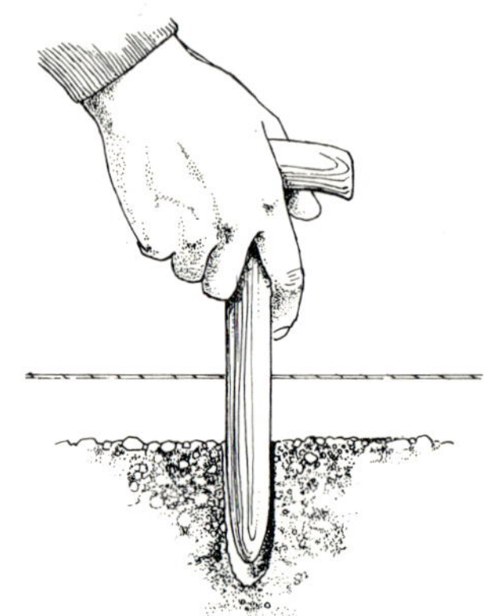

Put the line in position and make planting holes with dibber or trowel, preferably the latter in heavy soil, where the dibber tends to leave a compacted surface round the outside of the hole which discourages the spread of roots. Make

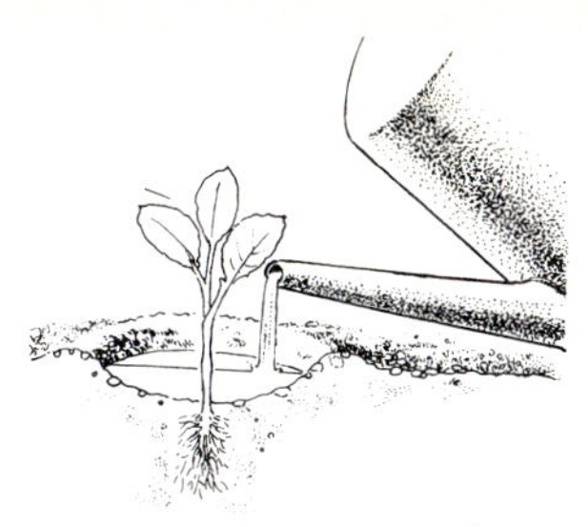

the hole deep enough to take the plant almost up to its lower leaves. Press the soil firmly around the roots and give the plant a drink of water before completely filling the hole.

In persistently dry weather, when continued watering may be necessary, plant in the bottom of a wide drill made with a draw hoe. Watering is then a simple matter of flooding the drill from hose or can, knowing that all the soil around the plants will be uniformly soaked. The drill, of course, gradually disappears with inter-row hoeing.

Keep a watch on newly planted brassicas for bird damage. It is an odd fact that plants which have remained unmolested in the seed-bed may be savagely attacked when they appear in a different place.

Leeks The same planting methods described above apply to most crops, but one, the leek, is treated a little differently. The plants are trimmed when taken from the seed-bed, long drooping leaves being cut back to half their length. The planting hole is made with the dibber, deep enough to take the plant with only 2cm or so above the surface. Insert the plant and fill the hole with water. This washes down enough soil to cover the roots, but otherwise the hole is left unfilled. The growing stem is in this way given a better chance to expand.

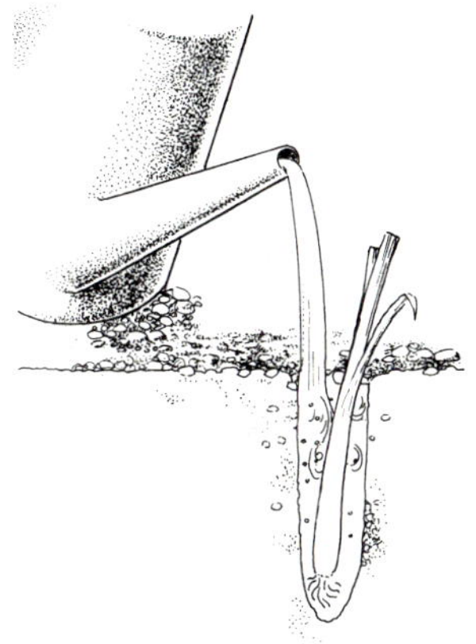

Tender crops A crucial factor when planting glass-raised plants in the open is timing. Nothing is gained by planting too early, a late frost can be disastrous, and low day temperatures with cold winds can cause a severe check especially to tomatoes.

Choose a sheltered and sunny position for the less hardy crops. Harden them off after removal from the greenhouse before planting out, standing them in the frame with daily less protection from the light until it is open day and night. In the event of bad weather after planting out, protect the plants in any way possible, cloching them, covering with plastic or, in the case of short plants like marrows and cucumbers, popping flower pots over them at night.

Marrows and cucumbers dislike root disturbance and move best when grown singly in pots. Make the planting hole on the prepared site and knock out the plant carefully from its pot, having watered it well beforehand. To remove the plant, hold the pot upside-down in the palm of the hand with the plant projecting downwards between the fingers. Tap the pot rim smartly on a hard surface and pot and plant will separate smoothly

Peat pots, which eliminate all root disturbance, should also be watered before planting out, the pot itself being well soaked. Bury the pot completely when planting to hasten its disintegration and the outward spread of roots.

Tomatoes are more tolerant of transplanting than the marrow tribe, but pot-grown plants are now usual. Tall tomato varieties should be staked and tied immediately after planting outdoors and the systematic removal of side-shoots begun at the same time.

◀ Knocking out a plant.

▼ Staking tomato plants.

FRUIT

The nursery catalogue Catalogues are available by early summer. Try to supplement them by visiting nurseries, noting the forms and sizes of mature trees, and discussing varieties and suitable rootstocks before placing an order in good time for autumn delivery.

Top fruit Fruit trees, if wisely chosen, and given a little regular attention, should crop for at least 20–30 years as compared with the 2–10 years of the soft fruits. Buying trees is thus naturally a little more complicated than buying bushes and canes.

Shape of tree The size and shape of the tree is important in the smaller garden where space is at a premium. For apples and pears the most suitable forms are the single cordon and the dwarf bush, and for peaches and nectarines the fan-trained varieties. Bush and pyramid trees are free-standing and require only minimal pruning; cordons and fan-trained trees are grown on the wall or some form of support, and need systematic but quite simple pruning.

Other forms of tree will be found in the catalogue, but those suggested are likely to give the best results in the average garden. Large, slow-maturing standards and half-standards are trees for the paddock or orchard.

In talking about the size of a tree we mean, of course, its size at maturity. On purchase, it will be 2–3 years old and still quite small. Don't buy older and larger trees; they take longer to recover from the move and the first crop may well be delayed rather than advanced. It is much cheaper to buy maidens. A maiden is just a single stem, one year's growth. It involves you in starting from scratch and building up a framework of branches—a fascinating task although it provides no immediate contribution to the table.

Rootstocks The stocks or roots on which cultivated fruits are grafted largely determine the size of the mature tree and the time it takes to come into bearing. A rootstock which encourages limited growth, fruitfulness and early maturity is known as a 'dwarfing' stock, and is the most suitable for garden trees.

Shapes of trees

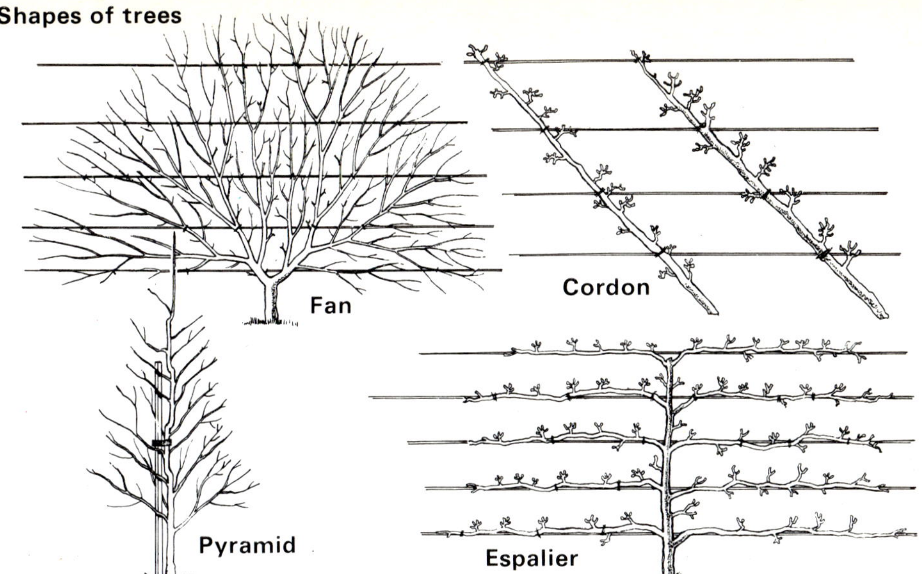

A reliable nurseryman's or fruit specialist's advice should be sought on this subject, because the choice of stock is influenced by the fertility of your soil.

Pollinators and choice of varieties Many varieties are self-sterile and cannot bear fruit unless fertilized by pollen from another variety. The catalogue will specify the self-sterile varieties and will probably indicate suitable pollinators for them—varieties flowering at about the same time.

If there are fruit trees within insect flight, the chances are that even a solitary self-sterile tree in your garden will fruit in a good season. But for one-tree plantings you should really stick to self-fertiles, which include some of the finest varieties like the Victoria Plum and Conference Pear. Though even they crop better with another variety nearby.

The family tree This consists of several, usually three, varieties worked on the one root. Apples and pears are available in this form and the idea is a perfectly practicable attempt to grow several varieties in a very small space, though the same object might be better achieved by planting three single stem cordons.

The family tree, which is in bush form, needs careful watching and pruning to prevent one stronger growing variety taking over the entire tree almost unnoticed.

SOFT FRUIT

Fruit bushes are planted when dormant, between late autumn and early spring. Autumn planting is generally preferable and to ensure delivery in time for this and to be sure of getting what you want, it is again wise to order early. It is sometimes a case of first come, best served, and the bargain offers of late winter, sold off to clear the land, are not the pick of the stock. The numbers of bushes or canes needed can be worked out from the table. Plant at the wider spacings where possible, especially with varieties known to be vigorous, but when aiming at optimum yield from a limited space, as in a fruit cage, keep to the closer of the recommended spacings.

Many soft fruits are prey to virus diseases, those most at risk being raspberries, loganberries, blackcurrants and strawberries. It is most important to deal with a reputable nursery, and where schemes of inspection and certification are applicable, to insist on certified stock. Virus diseases are not swift killers; they cause progressive stunting, malformation and falling yields, and long before symptoms are noticed the infection is being spread by insects such as aphids.

PLANTING

Trees Planting is possible any time during the dormant season from autumn to spring, provided the soil is not waterlogged or frozen hard. Soon after leaf-fall, while the soil is still warm, is the best time, but early delivery is only assured by early ordering.

Dig the planting site thoroughly, removing perennial weeds. Work in a couple of handfuls of bone meal per tree and a little well-rotted manure or compost. Store some soil under cover to be used at planting time if the conditions are very wet. Have ready stakes and ties for all trees not to be planted against a wall. On delivery, leave the trees wrapped if planting is likely in the near future, storing the package in a cool shed, not in a centrally heated house.

The day before planting, unwrap, soak the roots in water for 12 hours if they are dry and cut back any damaged or broken ones to the undamaged part. If planting is to be delayed, the trees should be temporarily heeled in. Dig a trench deep enough to take the roots when the trees are placed in it leaning against the side. Fill in the trench heaping plenty of soil over the roots. Trees may be safely left heeled in for weeks or even months.

In planting, begin by standing the tree upright on the site with the roots fully spread out. Mark round the outer limits of the roots with the spade as a guide to the size of the planting hole. Dig the hole deep enough for the tree to be planted at its former depth as shown by the soil mark on the stem. Break up the subsoil at the bottom of the hole.

Stand the tree in the hole, roots spread out, and fill in with the finest and most friable soil obtainable, sifting it between the roots and ramming it carefully and frequently with a light wooden rammer. If the tree is a free-standing bush or pyramid, insert the supporting stake as soon as enough soil has been filled in to hold the tree upright, driving it firmly into the subsoil. Complete the infilling and mulch the tree with peat or compost to reduce the penetration of frost. Tie it to the stake, which should be about 10cm from the stem, with an adjustable tie. No matter how small the tree, staking should never be deferred. It cannot establish itself if rocked and loosened by wind.

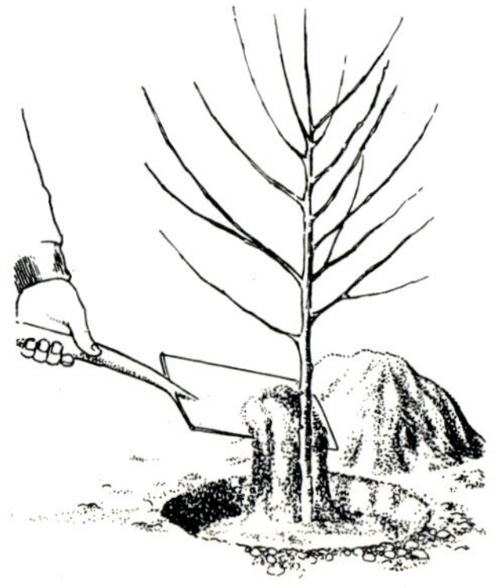

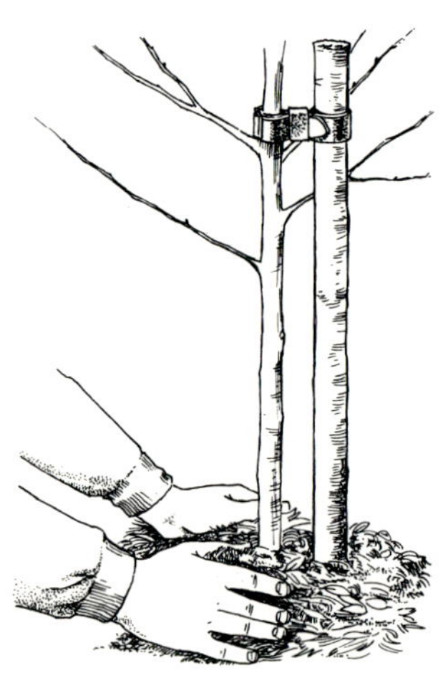

The planting holes for wall trees must be clear of the footings, which may leave the stem some 20cm from the wall. The stem, in the case of the cordon, and the branches on either side of the fan-trained tree, should be tied to bamboo canes until long enough to

Planting a cordon

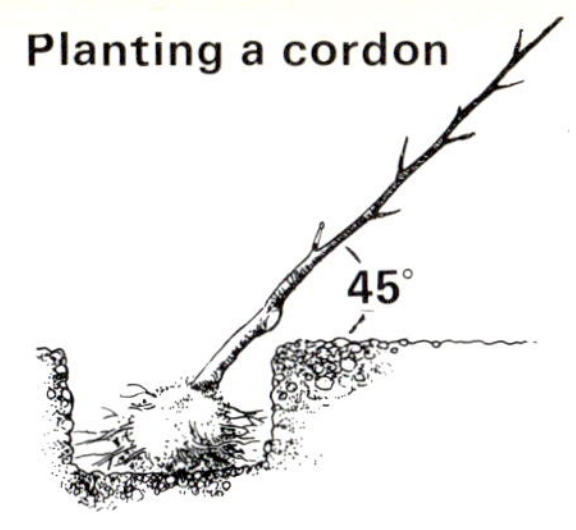

reach the wall and be permanently tied in. Cordons are planted with the stem slanting at an angle of 45 degrees which slows down growth and encourages the production of fruiting spurs. Cordons on house walls may have to be trained vertically later—to avoid a window, for instance—but should always start at an oblique angle.

Bushes Prepare ground for all soft fruit by thorough digging and cleaning, working in some rotted manure or compost and giving a good sprinkling of bone meal.

The principal soft fruits grown as bushes are gooseberries, red and white currants and blackcurrants. The same general rules on treatment and planting apply to bushes as to trees, but planting holes are of course shallower and roots nearer the surface. Mulch with peat or compost, and after severe frost tread back bushes that have been loosened or lifted from the ground.

Gooseberries and red and white currants grow on a single stem or leg and are planted up to the soil mark. Any shoots or suckers from the base of the leg should be removed. Blackcurrants, on the other hand, are encouraged to make a mass of fibrous root with many shoots springing up from the ground. They are planted a little more deeply than previously grown so that a few buds are buried. The branches are cut back to 15cm above ground level to encourage strong new growth from the base. This means no crop in the first year, but it would in any case be scarcely worth having and failure to cut back after planting entails a greater loss of crop over the long term.

Canes The cane fruits include blackberries, loganberries, raspberries, and lesser-known hybrids such as the boysenberry.

Planting times and methods are as for bush fruits, but all the cane fruits should be cut back to about 15cm from ground level after planting. They fruit on canes of the previous year's growth, and the first priority after planting is to get the plant established and producing strong fruiting canes in its first growing season.

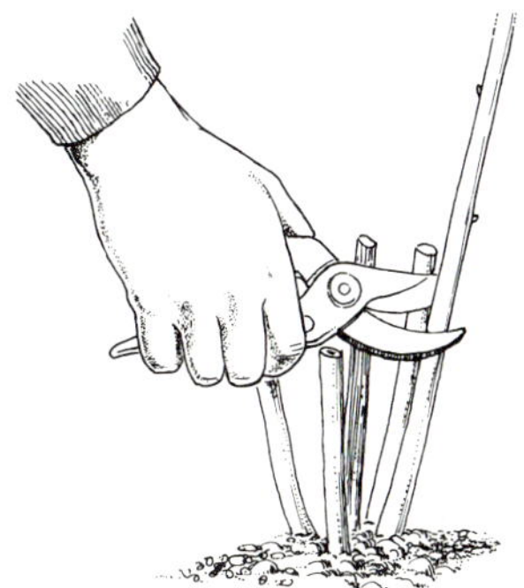

Remember when ordering that blackberries and loganberries need a lot of space and that the number of plants the average garden can accommodate is very limited. Provide permanent supports for the plants early in the summer after planting so that the young canes may be tied in position as they grow and before they get damaged.

Strawberry plants Summer-fruiting varieties are planted in late summer or early autumn, as soon as rooted runners are available. Early planting allows the plants to get established before the winter and makes all the difference to the following summer's crop. Plant with a trowel, spreading out the roots and making the plant very firm. The central bud should be just clear of the surface but all the

roots well covered. Water freely in dry weather.

Perpetual varieties are planted in early autumn or in spring. In the latter case, all blossoms are removed until mid-summer, when the first fruits may be allowed to set.

Cultivating vegetables

Between sowing or planting and the eventual harvest come a lot of routine operations which are all easy enough if they are tackled in time. The trouble is that everything in the garden develops at an alarming speed between late spring and late summer, and today's five-minute job is next week's major headache. The answer is to do a little and often.

Thinning

The use of pelleted seed greatly simplifies thinning, but many popular varieties are not yet available pelleted. Most crops are still grown from ordinary seed and, given good germination, thinning is essential, especially for root crops.

Thin in stages and start early before the seedlings become entangled. Never thin to the final distance at one fell swoop; casualties among seedlings are inevitable, and you may end up with a row which has more gaps than plants.

Thin when the soil is moist so that seedlings are withdrawn with minimum disturbance to those that remain. Water beforehand if necessary, but give the tops time to dry or the job will be unpleasantly messy. Thin to about 2cm apart at the first stage, then to twice that distance, then to the final spacing. In some crops—carrots, beetroot and turnips, for instance, the thinnings from the final stages could be large enough to use. The same applies to lettuce, the tender unhearted leaves being very acceptable in the salad bowl.

Care should be taken when thinning carrots not to attract the carrot fly, whose larvae badly damage the roots. It lays its eggs when attracted by the smell of the

plants as they are disturbed or crushed during thinning, which is best done in the evening when fewer of the insects are flying. Firm the soil carefully round the remaining plants and remove all the thinnings.

The important thing in the initial thinning of small seedlings is to achieve effective singling, to make sure that what you believe to be one plant is not in fact a clump of two or three. Beetroot are notoriously difficult because each beet 'seed' is really a dried fruit containing several seeds. No matter how thinly sown they come up in groups.

Weed control

The operative word is 'control'. Weeds can never be eliminated and the struggle is to keep them in check. Allow them to get on top and the crop is soon being starved of light, nutrients and water at a critical time.

Hand weeding

The simplest way to get rid of weeds is to pull them up. It is an effective method if they are small, not deeply rooted, and in moist or friable soil. It is also the only way to deal with weeds in actual crop rows and here it must be done with the least possible disturbance to the crop. Jerk the weed out smartly with one hand while pressing down the soil on either side of it with the other. That way you will not pull up adjoining soil and seedlings. If large, massively-rooted weeds like the annual sow thistle get established in the row, cut through the root with a trowel just below the surface and pull out the top.

◀ Hoeing between rows keeps weeds at bay.

Weeds with deep tap roots like docks and dandelions can be neatly removed by driving in the spade vertically close to the plant and levering it back until you feel the root snap. The plant then pulls with most of the root and is unlikely to reappear.

Hoeing

Frequent hoeing is the most effective way of controlling weeds between rows and in other open ground. If the surface is dry, the more often you hoe the better. Hoe while the weeds are small or, ideally, before they are visible. Weed seeds are always germinating just below the surface, so if you keep disturbing them in infancy annual weeds will not become a problem.

Use the draw hoe by taking short, steady strokes, drawing the blade towards you with the edge just under the surface, and walking forwards. The Dutch hoe is used with a forward stroke as you walk backwards. Keep the blade at only a slight angle to the ground so that the cultivation is very shallow. Go deeper, and you will bring up more dormant weed seeds to a level that encourages germination. Don't chop with the draw hoe or jab with the Dutch hoe, especially close to the crop row.

Herbicides

Herbicides or weedkillers are not a magic solution to the weed problem. Under the right conditions and properly applied, they are a useful additional tool.

The following are examples of the main types of herbicide used in the garden, the name of the active chemical being followed, where applicable, by a brand name.

Sodium chlorate Fatal to most vegetation, including the strongest perennial weeds, if used in sufficient strength. An effective weedkiller for paths and may be used on cultivated ground if a long enough interval is allowed between application and planting for the rain to wash it from the soil.

Paraquat (Weedol) A quick acting contact poison absorbed through the green parts of the plant. It breaks down and leaves no toxic effects on contact with the

Using herbicides

Herbicides are dangerous if handled improperly. Apply from a can fitted with a rose or sprinkler bar, not from a sprayer. It is essential to keep a special can for the purpose, plainly labelled or distinctively coloured. Disastrous consequences ensue if an unwashed herbicide can is used for watering.

Store packets and bottles of herbicide out of reach of small children and not in the greenhouse.

Mix only enough solution for the job in hand. Flush any surplus down the drain. Don't retain left-over solution for future use and, above all, *never, never* store it in soft drink or similar bottles.

soil, which may be sown or planted immediately after its use. Very effective against all annual and some perennial weeds if used in bright, dry weather.

2,4,5,T (Nettlekiller, Brushwood Killer) A selective or hormone herbicide, destroying broad-leaved weeds but not grasses. Clears nettles and creeping thistles if applied when they are in full growth. No long-term effect on soil but should not be used near tomatoes, or on ground they are to occupy that season, or be kept in a greenhouse where they are growing.

Dalapon (Dowpon) Another selective herbicide effective against grass weeds. Used as directed and combined with good cultivation, it can eliminate couch or twitch, though it must be added that repeated digging and hand picking of the underground stems in summer will do so just as well.

Watering

The soil accumulates water during the winter, the season of heavy rainfall and minimum growth. But in the average summer there will be times when lack of moisture is a limiting factor on yields, and then something must be done to supplement and conserve it.

The moisture deficit

Soil moisture is lost during the growing season in two ways, by direct evaporation from the surface and by transpiration from plants.

The first is only a limited loss, but loss by transpiration may have to be made up artificially, because the larger the plant the more water it takes up from the soil, and the warmer and drier the weather the faster it loses moisture from the leaves. The crop may thus suffer from lack of water when it is approaching maturity, and under greatest stress, when tubers or fruit swell and pods form.

The amount of water likely to be needed cannot be quantified. It varies with the state of the soil in spring and conditions during the growing period. With an average rainfall of 6cm per month, most crops will benefit from watering as they approach maturity. With less rain the moisture deficit in the soil increases and yields are affected.

Rainfall of 2cm equals 4 litres per sq m so if there was negligible rainfall for a month some 30–40 litres per sq m would be needed merely to keep the deficit within normal limits, and this is some guide to the quantities required for effective watering.

Water does not reach the lower levels of soil until the upper layer is saturated. It is useless giving a little water and expecting it to work its way down; it is more likely to attract roots nearer to the surface where

▲ In a dry month 30–40 litres of water are required per square metre.

they are at greater risk from drying out. Soak a small area thoroughly and don't waste water on perfunctory splashings all over the place.

Mulching

A mulch is any material spread on the soil to reduce evaporation. If it consists of compost or rotted manure, it has some nutritive value; if of peat it improves the soil when eventually dug in. These organic mulches should be applied when the soil is wet and spread close to both sides of the crop row in strips 4–6cm deep and as wide as circumstances permit.

Although organic matter makes the best mulch, other

materials, such as stones, serve to retain moisture. Black polythene is more practical. Weighted down with soil or stones it conserves moisture and suppresses weeds. If you grow bush tomatoes under cloches, try putting down a strip of it and planting through slits cut at required spacings. Water by inserting the can or hose under the edge of the polythene. This means less watering, no

weeds, and a clean resting place for the fruit. Try it also with strawberries.

Cheapest and simplest of all is the soil mulch, the shallow layer of loose soil produced by constant hoeing. Because the soil particles are loose they block the upward movement of moisture by capillary action, and because the ground is kept weed-free there are fewer plants to suck it up and lose it by transpiration.

Supporting plants

Some crops are natural climbers, others are better described as floppers. Both types are better for some kind of support to keep them from contact with the soil.

Runner beans

The runner is a true climber, twining readily round any kind of support. It may be dwarfed by pinching on the growing point at a height of 45cm and doing the same with the laterals as they develop to produce a bush, but the pods are less straight and in wet seasons may be dirty and slug-eaten. Larger crops are produced from climbers.

The best bean poles are 2m bamboo canes, which last for years if stored in the dry after the crop is cleared. Beans are liable to wind damage, and a row heavy

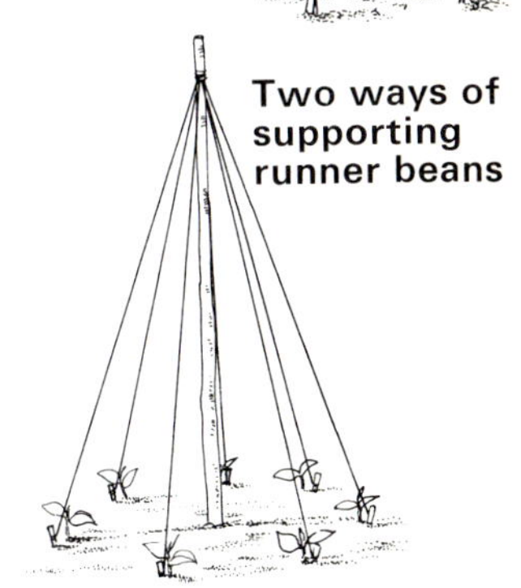

Two ways of supporting runner beans

with leaves and pods may be completely wrecked by a broadside wind. As an alternative to the row, grow them on a wigwam or tepee. Mark out a square with 1m sides. Insert bamboos 30cm apart and 15cm deep along the sides, gather the canes together at the top and tie them firmly. Sow two or three seeds at the foot of each cane. The structure is very stable; at least two sides are always out of the wind, and in capacity the square metre equals a 4m row.

Peas

Tall varieties and the necessary peasticks have virtually disappeared, but the dwarf forms now universally grown need something to keep them clear of wet ground where the pods are apt to rot.

Get a ball of thick garden twine and some stout canes or light wooden stakes about 70cm long. When the peas are about 8cm tall, insert the stakes down both sides of the row 8cm away from it and 120cm apart. Run a horizontal string, 15cm from the ground round the row, pulled taut as it encircles each stake. Make it fast at the end and run a second strand 30cm higher. A third may be added later if necessary. The peas grow enclosed in a neat string fence which prevents them flopping. The stakes and even the string may be used repeatedly.

Dwarf beans

When carrying a heavy crop the plants often topple over in stormy weather, and dirty and damaged pods again result. Earth up the stems as the plants grow and support heavy clusters of pods with forked twigs.

Tomatoes

Tall varieties outdoors must be secured to good stakes or canes or to hooks or eyes in a wall or fence. Under glass

the simplest method is stringing. Attach a length of twine to a roof glazing bar or timber and to a peg in the ground near the plant. It may even be tied round the base of the tomato stem, but this needs some care. As the plant grows it is gently twisted round the string and no tying is necessary.

Dwarf beans

Pollinating a marrow

Pollination

The fertilization of vegetable crops presents no serious problems, as it does in the case of fruit. In a few crops, however, yields are sometimes reduced by pollination failures.

Marrows, courgettes and squashes

The plants bear separate male and female flowers, the latter easily identifiable by the baby fruit immediately behind the flower. If pollen is not transferred from a male flower, the fruitlet will not swell but will decay and drop off. If this happens when the plant carries both male and female flowers, try hand pollination. Pick a newly-opened male flower early in the morning, strip off the petals and insert it into a female flower with the pollen covered anther in contact with the stigma. Leave it in position and repeat with other flowers as they open.

Cucumbers

Basically the same as the marrow family. Outdoor varieties must be fertilized, but hand pollination is unnecessary. Indoor varieties are better not pollinated; the fruit develops without it and pollination leads to the production of seeds and bitter, mis-shapen fruit. Pick off all male blooms or grow a variety like Femspot, which bears mainly female flowers.

▲ Growing tomatoes by the ring culture method.

Sweetcorn

Fertilization occurs when the sticky 'silk' which hangs from the end of the cob catches pollen falling from the tassel 'x' at the top of the plant.

If planted in a single row, much of the pollen may be blown away by a cross-wind and the cobs incompletely fertilized. Plant in a block of short rows, with rows and plants equidistant, and the wind-borne pollen has a much better chance of being caught by the silk.

GROWING IN CONTAINERS

Growing crops in containers, whether outdoors, under glass, or in small pots for subsequent planting, has special problems.

Watering

In the greenhouse where frequent attention is impossible, the capillary sand tray is a solution for small pots. They stand on a bed of damp sand fed from a reservoir below, and although overhead watering remains necessary, the possibility of complete disaster is reduced. Other automatic watering systems for the greenhouse, and the various forms of self-watering pot should also be considered. Specifically for greenhouse tomatoes, another possibility is ring culture. Here, a deep bed of fine washed ballast, or crushed clinker, or peat is laid down on the floor or staging. On it stand 'tom-pots', whalehide cylinders filled with potting compost, in which the tomatoes are planted. They soon root through into the material below, which is kept well watered, liquid feed being given only in the potting compost. The plants manage with a daily watering, compared with the three or four per day necessary in hot weather when grown in a 25 or 30cm pot.

As to pot-grown plants outdoors it should be remembered that only heavy and continuous rain renders watering unnecessary. Showers which damp the topsoil have no effect on pots.

Growing bags

First developed by tomato growers as an alternative to sterilization or replacement of greenhouse soil, the growing bag consists of a sort of plastic bolster filled with a peat-based growing medium. Laid flat with a planting slit opened along the top, it takes from two to four tomato plants. At first glance it seems not to have the depth or capability for such a crop, but extraordinary yields—up to 28kg a plant—have been claimed for growing bag tomatoes. They may be used for other crops, under glass or in the open.

It is essential that the growing medium be kept quite wet, one test suggested being that the surface should always be moist enough to soak a piece of newspaper pressed on it. As a precaution against waterlogging small slits should be cut in the side of the bag 2cm above the ground.

Cultivating fruit

Perhaps the most satisfying garden product is fresh fruit and contrary to popular opinion fruit growing does not necessarily require acres of space. Readily available are quick-maturing trees or dwarfing stock and you can choose from a wide selection of cordon and fan-trained varieties.

For much of the time fruits look after themselves, not needing the intensive care demanded by vegetables. Routine work is spread over the year and fruit gives a generous return on time and labour.

THE CARE OF NEW PLANTINGS

Top Fruit

The importance of securing the young tree against wind movement has already been stressed. Rocking causes pockets of air or water to form round the roots and prevents their proper contact with the soil.

Apply a mulch in early spring to trees not mulched immediately after planting. Peat is as good as manure or compost, the manurial value being unimportant and the sole object to conserve moisture. Spread the material around the tree as far as you remember the roots extending at planting.

Watering will be necessary if a dry summer follows planting, even with the protection of a mulch. Make sure the soil does not get really dry and pay special attention to wall trees, which often need a good soaking when well established. In very hot, sunny weather, newly planted trees should be sprayed overhead in the evenings.

Trees should not be allowed to fruit in the first season after planting. Blossom and any fruits that have set should be picked off.

Soft fruit

Autumn plantings must be examined throughout the winter for signs of frost-lifting. Late-planted strawberries are the most likely victims, and after a hard frost may be found squeezed up from the ground on a pillar of root.

From spring onwards all bushes and canes will need the same care in regard to watering as the tree fruits.

The cane fruits—raspberries, blackberries and loganberries—and blackcurrants, all of which were cut back to 15cm on planting, must be encouraged to make as much growth as possible to crop the following season. Growth is helped by an application of 100g per sq m of a compound fertilizer lightly forked in before mulching. Blackcurrants always seem to need nitrogen and this fertilizer dressing should be repeated annually unless you can mulch them with animal manure.

Summer-fruiting strawberries planted on well prepared soil in late summer or early autumn need no special treatment and should bear a moderate crop of large berries. Plants intended for cloching should be covered as soon as they start to grow and must thereafter be watered with increasing frequency as the fruit sets and swells.

Perpetual varieties planted in autumn may be allowed to carry a few summer fruits but spring-planted ones must be de-blossomed. In both cases the real crop is carried in autumn, and although the plants at first look small and miserable, they end up as robust, sprawling clumps, even fruiting on the unrooted runners.

PRUNING

The three main aims of pruning are to maintain the proper shape of the tree, to remove dead, diseased or unwanted wood, and to promote the growth of fruit-bearing wood.

Essential tools are a pair of secateurs for small trees and soft fruits, a pruning saw for larger branches, a long-handled pruner for tall, neglected trees, stout gloves for loganberries and blackberries, and a sharp pruning knife. The last is valuable for trimming untidy saw cuts which are often entry points for disease; you cannot satisfactorily paint the stump of a branch if it bristles with broken snags after sawing.

Cordon apples and pears

The aim is to produce a main stem thickly studded with short laterals and fruiting spurs, the stubby growths bearing clusters of fruit buds. A tree pruned in winter is stimulated into more vigorous growth, but pruning young shoots in summer checks growth and causes the tree to produce more fruit buds. Begin by summer-pruning the laterals, pinching out the growing points when they have three clusters of leaves, usually about mid-summer. In winter, prune the laterals back further to 5cm of new growth The leading shoot of the main stem is not stopped in summer, but the new growth is cut back by one third in winter. Winter pruning must not be carried out in hard frost and should be completed as soon as possible after leaf-fall.

Dwarf bush apples

The form has a short stem or trunk from which branches grow upwards and outwards, leaving the centre open. Prune each branch as though it were a cordon, cutting back the laterals and reducing the length of the leaders. Allow more main branches to grow up if there is room, but remove any growing inwards and keep the centre clear. As much light as possible should reach every branch, for there appears to be a direct relation between fruitfulness and exposure to sunlight.

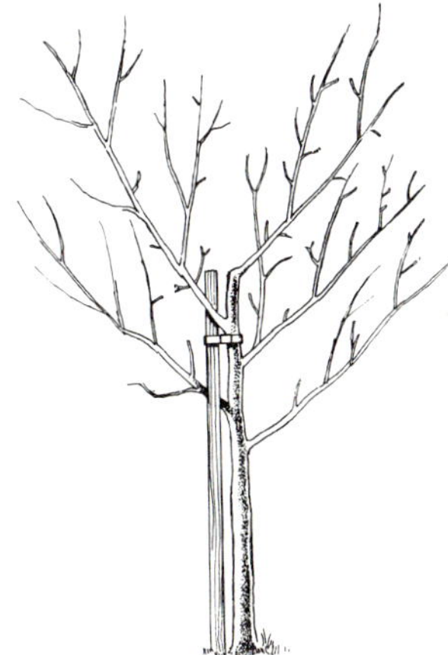

Bush plums

Plums, like all stone fruit, should be pruned as little as possible, and bush trees may be left to grow more or less naturally. Remove dead and diseased branches and any that are rubbing and chafing against others. Do any necessary pruning in the summer when wounds heal more quickly, and cover all cut surfaces of more than 1cm diameter with bituminous paint or the anti-fungal paint obtainable from garden shops. The spores of the very destructive silver leaf disease gain entry through open wounds.

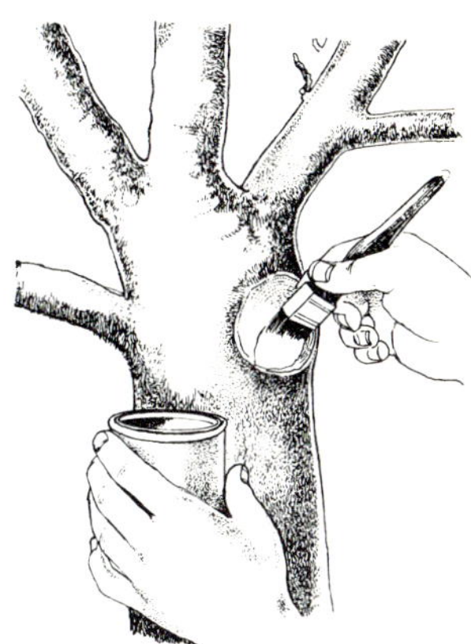

Peaches and nectarines

These fruits are usually grown as fan-trained trees on walls, and being basically the same are pruned in the same way

Fruit is borne on shoots made the previous year. Several such shoots will be found growing from the base of the current year's fruit-bearing shoot. Nip them all out but one during the summer, leaving the one 'replacement shoot' to grow on. In the autumn, cut out the old fruiting shoot and tie in the replacement.

The main branches are allowed to extend into the available wall space and the object of pruning is to regulate the number of young shoots and prevent the tree becoming a dense mass of growth.

Soft fruit: bushes

Red and white currants and gooseberries produce fruiting spurs like apples. Trim back the laterals each year to within 6–7cm of the main branches. Shorten the new wood of the leading shoots at the tips of the branches by a third, and in the case of gooseberries with long drooping branches by a half. These bushes are grown on a short 'leg' and this must be kept free of any growths below the main branches and of suckers from the ground.

Blackcurrants are entirely different. They fruit most freely on young branches springing up from the ground, and to encourage a thicket of these about a quarter of the older branches are cut out annually just above ground level. Remove those with the oldest, darkest and hardest wood. It is possible to regenerate a neglected bush by cutting the whole thing down to the ground and giving it plenty of nitrogen.

Soft fruit: canes

The pruning of the cane fruits is simplicity itself. They fruit on growth made the previous year. The current year's fruiting canes are cut out immediately the crop is gathered and the new canes trained in their place. It is important to provide the new growth with space and light to mature and ripen the wood before winter. The long-caned varieties like blackberries are more easily managed if a space on the training supports is reserved for the new canes to be separated from the fruiting ones and tied in safe from possible breakage as they grow.

▼ Where to prune red and white currants.

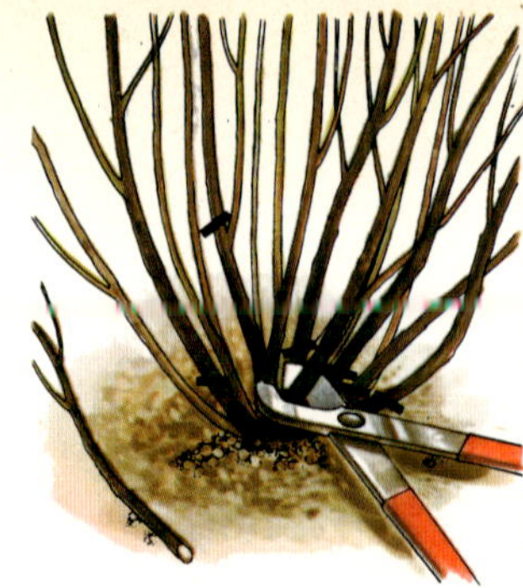

▲ Cutting out old fruiting canes of a blackberry bush.

FRUIT TREES IN POTS

The trees are quite small, grown on very dwarfing stocks, and are easily moveable. They are usually repotted annually and this entails a gradual increase in pot size. It also produces a mass of fibrous root which encourages regular cropping under artificial conditions.

The trees may stand in a courtyard or anywhere open to full light. Continuous direct sunlight is not essential, but a balcony with an opaque roof is ruled out.

In winter, the trees are best left outdoors and protective material placed round the pots to prevent the compost freezing solid. On no account should they be

brought into artificial warmth, though in spring they may be placed in the cold greenhouse for a time to protect the blossom from frost.

PROTECTION FROM BIRDS

Some form of specific action must be taken to prevent bird damage to fruit, especially to soft fruit, or you may lose the entire crop. However, the birds may be less determined robbers if you increase their drinking facilities and place shallow pans of water at strategic points, and if you also feed them. The soft fruit season is the thirstiest time of the year, and some species will be struggling to feed a second brood. A little assistance does not make bird-proof netting unnecessary, but it makes the recipients a little less diligent in seeking holes in it.

Top fruit

The worst problem is not damage to the fruit itself, but the destruction of fruit buds in early spring by bullfinches. Preventive measures suggested include covering the trees with netting or growing them in fruit cages. The latter idea is increasingly practised in the case of apples, dwarf bush trees on M9 stocks being quite small enough when mature to function in a cage two metres high. Unfortunately, no equally dwarfing stock exists for other fruits.

▲ A healthy example of a fan-trained apple tree.

The fruit cage

A bird-proof enclosure for apple trees may be an extravagance, but for the soft fruits something of the sort, permanent or temporary, is a necessity.

The size of a permanent cage depends on available ground and resources, and also on your choice of fruits. Cooking gooseberries need no protection, but for dessert varieties it is essential. —so is it for strawberries, raspberries and loganberries. Blackberries are sometimes at risk and sometimes ignored. They take up a lot of space, and a cage should really be planted to yield the maximum crop from the area. On this criterion, raspberries are perhaps the most profitable.

The cage will have to be adapted to the site. Construction may be of timber uprights at 2m intervals, the sides covered with 2cm mesh wire netting. A batten should run along the top of the uprights, and over this be drawn the top covering of nylon netting, removed after cropping to give birds free access in winter and replaced just before fruiting the following season.

The top netting is secured to hooks on the uprights and horizontal batten, and to keep it from sagging wires may be stretched from side to side, with central supporting posts in the case of a very wide cage.

A permanent roof of wire netting is not recommended. It prevents the entry of birds when their activities are beneficial. It is heavy and needs additional internal support. Wet snow can accumulate on it and the weight may wreck the whole structure. And there is evidence that the drip from new galvanized wire netting is harmful to foliage.

The bottom of the netting must be made bird-tight, either by burying a few centimetres after giving an extra protective coating of bitumen paint, or by stapling to a base-board. Birds, especially blackbirds, usually find their way in at ground level. The door of the cage should be well fitting and wide enough to take a barrow.

Temporary protection

More limited protection than that afforded by the fruit cage is easy with nylon netting which is small-meshed, strong and durable.

Assume that you want to protect a row of raspberries. You will need a piece of netting somewhat longer than the row, and wide enough to cover it with a margin of space at the top and sides, two bamboo canes for every metre of row, about 30cm longer than the height of the raspberries, and a small jam or fish paste jar for each bamboo.

Insert the bamboos at 120cm intervals along both sides of the row and well clear of it. Place a jar on the top of each. Peg one edge of the netting down along the outside of one row of bamboos, then pull it up, over the top and down the other side. It will slide smoothly over the jars without catching or tearing and may be pulled taut, then pegged or weighted down. The surplus at the ends is gathered together and also pegged down.

The temporary cage is removed and packed away after the crop is gathered and will last for many years.

Strawberries are protected in the same way but the supports need only be 60cm high. It is useless merely to throw netting over strawberry plants. The birds sit on it, weigh it down and peck the berries through it. Unripe fruit grows through the mesh and is pulled off when the net is lifted for picking.

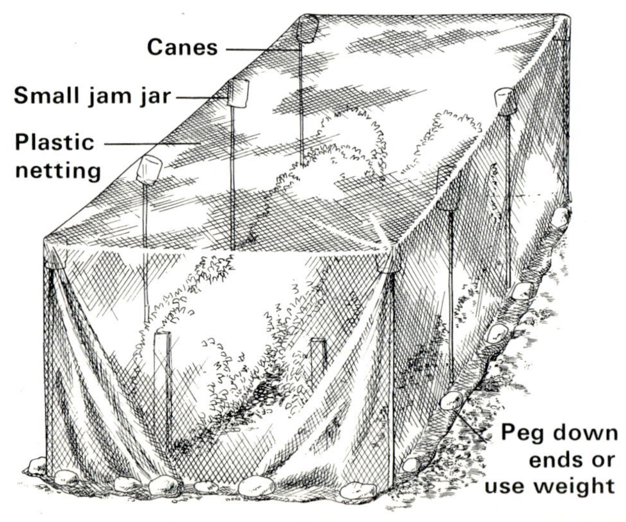

SUPPORTING CANE FRUIT

Raspberries

The canes must be supported if they are not to flop all over the place, damaging the fruit and young canes and rendering inter-row cultivation impossible. The conventional method is to have stout posts at the ends of the row carrying three horizontal strands of plastic-coated fencing wire at 40cm intervals, the first at 40cm from the ground. The wires must be strained tight, and in a long row some light intermediate posts will be necessary. Canes are tied to wires as they grow and strong-growing varieties are trimmed off at 2m, 40cm above the top wire.

The above method results in a tidy job, but is time-consuming, especially as the new canes must be tied to the wires and the old ones cut away every year. A way of avoiding all ties is to have parallel wires about 5cm apart with the canes growing between them. Three pairs of wires may be used, spaced at 40cm as suggested for single ones, but a single pair 1m from the ground might be adequate for weak growers like Lloyd George.

Traditional method of supporting raspberries

Blackberries and loganberries

The long, spiny growths must be properly trained and secured, otherwise they will become almost impossible handle. If no fence or trellis is available, train them on a post and wire erection similar to the conventional raspberry arrangement but on a larger scale. The canes must not be crowded together and unless the new growth is kept separate from the fruiting canes it may get badly damaged during picking or when cutting out the old canes after fruiting.

As suggested in the reference to pruning, the canes may be trained first to one side of the plant and then to the other, the positions of the new and fruiting canes being reversed and each season starting with a clear space on which the young canes may be trained.

Fast-growing blackberries need a lot of space. To keep this to a minimum, the canes should be taken up as high as possible before being trained horizontally. The topmost supporting wire for the more vigorous blackberries, which may have canes 3m long, should be 175cm from the ground. This is about the maximum height for easy picking.

▼ Training cane fruit by taking new canes to one side of the plant and old canes to the other.

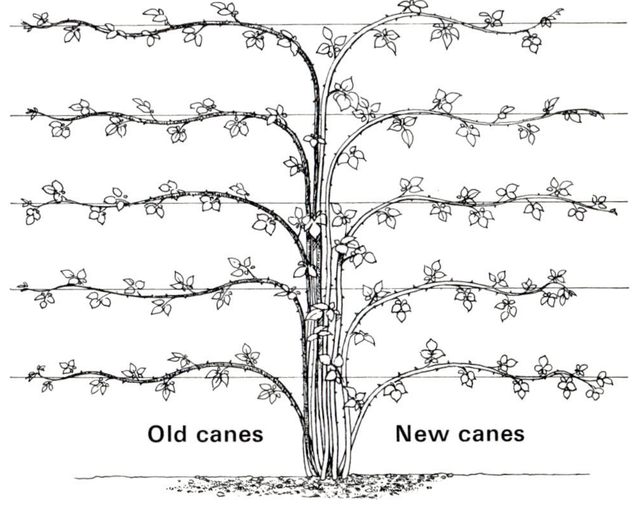

Gathering and storing

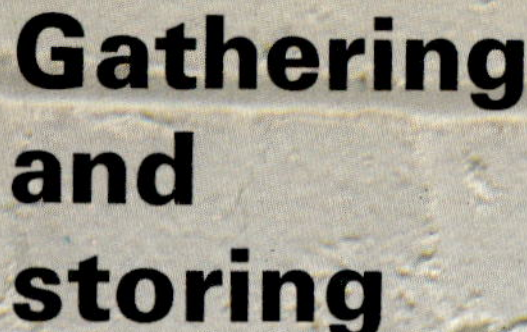

Gathering the crop should be the most satisfying part of garden routine. It can also be very important, affecting yields and quality in some crops if incorrectly carried out. If you have grown surplus produce accidentally or by design, then you can

store it in a variety of ways to provide food for the winter months. For freezing purposes vegetables have to be gathered at the right stage of growth and in perfect condition. Unless this is done, they may well deteriorate.

▼ A fine collection of home-grown produce proves that the gardener's labours are well worth-while.

VEGETABLES: ROOT CROPS

Potatoes

Lift and use early varieties only as required. Any remaining after the tops have dried may be stored like maincrops if left in the ground until the skins have 'set' and cannot be rubbed off by pressure of the thumb.

Lift healthy maincrops after the tops have died naturally, but if there are traces of blight, cut off, remove and burn the tops, leaving the tubers until the skins have set and if possible lift before heavy rains wash blight spores down to them.

Dig carefully, leave the tubers to dry for a few hours, remove damaged ones for immediate use, and store the rest in boxes in *complete* darkness and safe from frost. The smallest amount of light renders the tubers green and inedible and frost reduces them to pulp. Storage in clamps in the garden is unsuitable for small quantities and can lead to losses from frost and vermin.

Carrots

Pull young roots for immediate use and freezing as part of the thinning programme. Lift the maincrop carefully with a fork or spade in autumn, trim off the tops and gently clean the roots of soil. Discard any that are split or damaged and store in boxes covered with peat or sand in an unheated shed or outhouse. Inspect at intervals and remove roots with mould or disease.

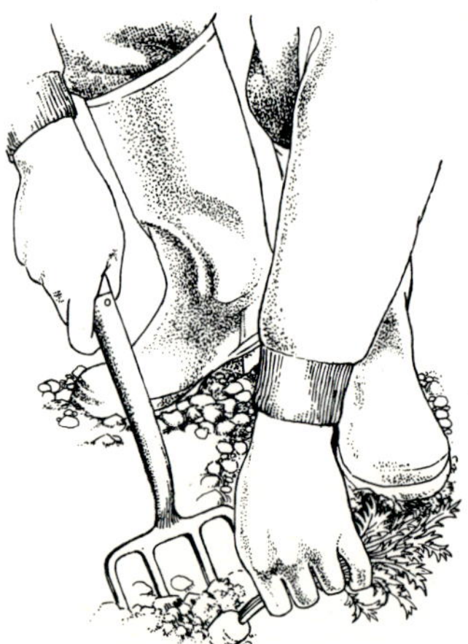

▶ Lifting maincrop carrots.

Beetroot

Treat as advised for carrots but take great care when lifting to avoid damage to the roots with consequent bleeding. Allow to wilt before twisting off the tops with the hands, do not cut them. Store in a cool place and safe from frost.

Turnips and swedes

May be lifted later than other root crops, and in mild winters late-sown turnips will continue to grow if left in the ground and pulled when needed. Any unused will shoot out and provide spring greens. Lifted roots may be stored in boxes covered with sacks. Peat or sand is unnecessary. Conditions should be very cool and slight frost will do no harm.

Onions

Bend the tops over in late summer to hasten ripening.

▼ Onions with their tops bent over.

Clean the bulbs after lifting, removing soil, roots, tops and loose skin. Dry very thoroughly, spreading the bulbs in a cool place, hanging in bunches or in bags of netting to keep them well ventilated and dry.

Parsnips

Leave in the ground and lift as required. If hard frost threatens cover with straw or other protective material to facilitate digging. Lift and store unused roots when growth restarts in early spring or the roots will soon be uneatable.

BRASSICA CROPS

Brussels sprouts

Begin picking at the base of the stem and upwards. Pick the top last of all, as earlier picking causes the remaining sprouts to 'blow' or open out.

Cabbages

If a few leaves are left on the

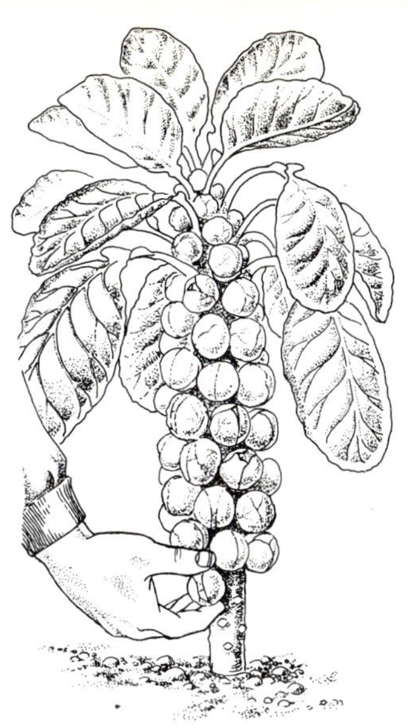

stump when the heart of a spring or summer cabbage is cut useful young shoots are produced. Don't leave them if grey cabbage aphis is present on the leaves—pull the stumps up and burn them.

Cabbages of the Winter White variety may be cut and stored for many weeks in a cool, dark place when standing crops are likely to be damaged by severe weather.

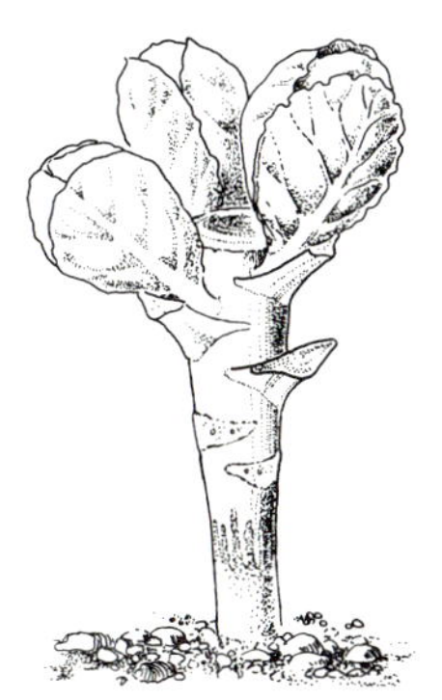

Cauliflowers
Summer crops tend to mature at the same time and the freezer is the best way of dealing with the surplus. Bend outer leaves over the maturing curds to prevent discolouration by the hot sun. If an entire plant is dug up by the roots and hung upside down in a cool shed the curd remains usable for up to a fortnight.

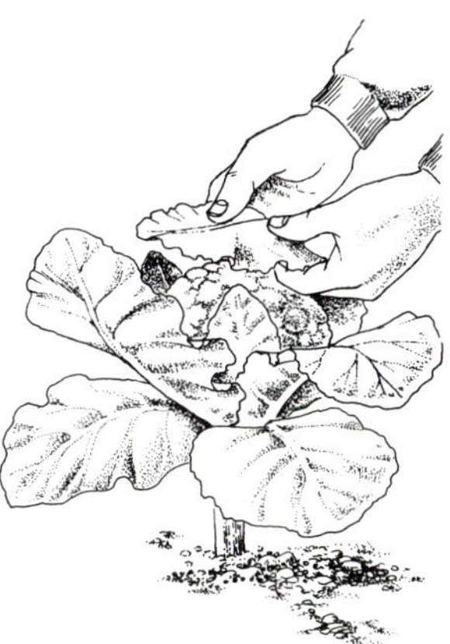

PEAS AND BEANS

All these crops must be picked over frequently and thoroughly and the pods used while young. Pods too old for use should still be picked unless they are to be left for seed, because once the seeds in a pod reach full size the plant loses its incentive to produce more and yield is diminished. Gather garden peas while the pods are smooth and green, sugar peas while the pods are flat and before the seeds form. The same applies to runner beans, which in hot weather should be picked over every other day.

Beans of the haricot type kept for winter use should be left on the vine until the pods are brown and crisp. Then shell them and spread out in a single layer in a dry, airy place for a week before storing in airtight jars.

OTHER CROPS

Marrows and squashes
Keep on cutting the fruit while young to prolong cropping. Marrows and winter squashes for storing must be left on the plant until fully ripe, their skin almost as hard as wood, and gathered before the first frost. Inspect very frequently when in store—the fruits have a nasty habit of decaying internally before you realize it.

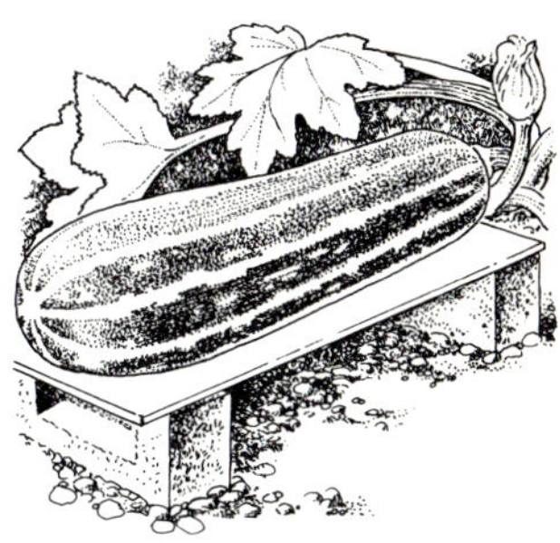

Tomatoes
The best fruit is fully ripened before picking. Unripe fruit at the end of the season will ripen if slightly coloured when picked, but the completely green ones are more doubtful. Keep them in warm conditions to ripen. Whether they are in sunlight or in the dark is immaterial and the only advantage of wrapping the fruit individually is that it prevents a decaying fruit infecting its neighbours.

FRUIT: TOP FRUIT

Apples and pears

These are the main fruits to be stored naturally as distinct from those requiring artificial preservation.

If you want fruit for winter you must grow keeping varieties. The catalogue will tell you the approximate season of use and probably when the variety should be

picked. A fruit is ready if it comes away with a very slight pull when lifted so that the stalk is horizontal. If it needs a tug it is not yet ready and will not keep well.

Store apples under cool conditions, preferably about 5°C. Wrap the fruit in special oiled paper wraps, squares of newspaper or ventilated polythene bags. Store well away from strong smelling substances like fresh paint.

Pears may be stored at a higher temperature than apples and are not usually wrapped. Dessert pears should be inspected almost daily when ripening.

▲ Branches sagging under the weight of plums should be propped up.

Plums

Support heavily laden branches with props to prevent breakage and the possible entry of disease. Fruit for jamming and bottling may be picked before fully ripe but dessert fruit must be allowed to ripen fully on the tree. Dessert gages are liable to split in wet weather and must then be picked even though unripe.

Peaches and nectarines

The fruit is easily damaged by rough handling. Test for ripeness by gentle pressure near the stalk, if the fruit 'gives' at that point it is ripe. Place in a single layer on a lining of soft material in the basket.

SOFT FRUIT

Blackcurrants

The berries are likely to be in better condition if the entire bunch is picked and the stalk or string removed later. The last few berries at the tip of the bunch may have to be discarded as unripe.

Gooseberries

Thin culinary varieties as they reach usable size, giving the rest more chance to

swell. Their thorns make gooseberries one of the less pleasant fruits to gather and in dealing with a large, crowded bush it may be quicker to pick with one hand and use the other, gloved, to hold up the branches.

Raspberries

Pick when fully ripe and the berry comes away easily from the white core. Pick when dry; damp raspberries go mouldy overnight.

Strawberries

The fruit should be uniformly coloured, with no unripe patches on shoulders or tip. Pick the plants over daily in hot weather, holding the berries by the stalk and handling them as little as possible.

Troubles and pests

The maintenance of healthy growth which will provide a natural resistance to pests and diseases is as important as quick action against these troubles when they arise. Regular inspection of your crops for caterpillars, insects, maggots, grubs, flies and eggs is the best way to forestall an all-out attack.

Feeding faults
Half-starved plants always seem to attract the nastiest bugs. Maintain soil fertility by digging in all the organic matter you can get hold of and supplementing it with fertilizers. But use these with discretion and do not over-apply.

Fruit trees, too, can suffer from over-feeding, though this usually results from planting in a soil that is just too fertile. If a young tree persists in making excessive growth and is reluctant to bear fruit stop cultivating round it and cover the ground with grass. Allow this to grow faily long, cutting it only two or three times each season, to take up some of the soil nitrogen. Don't try to reduce the tree's exuberance by hard pruning, this will only increase it.

Hygiene
Keep down all weed growth near the cultivated area. Neglected weed patches are sanctuaries for slugs and thistles, nettles and goose-grass are hosts for blackfly, which later migrate to broad and runner beans. Dispose of the remains of spent crops as soon as possible. Pull up and burn the stumps of winter brassicas, which often harbour cabbage aphis. Burn potato and tomato foliage affected by blight and diseased tubers and fruit. Burn all fruit prunings and any strawberry plants suspected of virus.

Practice crop rotation wherever possible as a precaution against soil-borne disease. The devastating outbreak of potato wart disease during World War I was attributed to the continuous growing of potatoes in gardens and allotments.

Functional troubles
Bolting, or premature running to seed, often results from a check to the plant's development. It may be caused by poor soil, lack of water, overcrowding from delayed thinning and adverse weather conditions.

Bolting spinach

With fertile soil and good cultivation most crops produce only the occasional bolter, but in a few instances, as with beetroot sown too early and checked by cold, a substantial part of the crop may bolt.

There is one variety, Boltardy, which is resistant to the trouble, but the general rule, also applicable to other crops, is not to sow too early in spring in cold districts.

Vegetable pests and diseases
Pesticides should be used with the same precautions as advised for herbicides. The safest are those derived from derris and pyrethrum, and these are obtainable as convenient aerosols or as dust in blower packs. Household aerosol fly sprays must not be used on plants.

ROOT CROPS

Potatoes
Virus diseases and eelworm: Plant only certified seed.

Wireworms and slugs: the first is a thin, yellowish soil pest often found in newly cultivated grassland, the second usually a small terrestrial species present in heavily manured land. Both bore holes in the tubers. Treat the ground with Bromophos or other soil pesticide guaranteed not to taint the crop.

Scab: brown excrescences of the skin of tubers and causing wastage in peeling. Some varieties are more susceptible than others but the trouble is often due to a too-alkaline soil. Surround the seed tubers with plenty of peat at planting time.

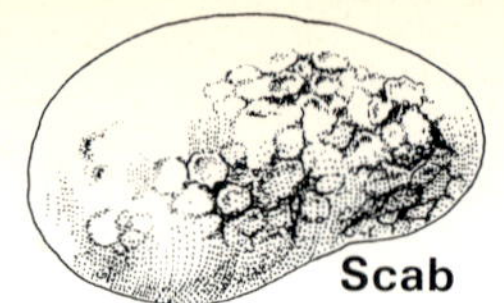

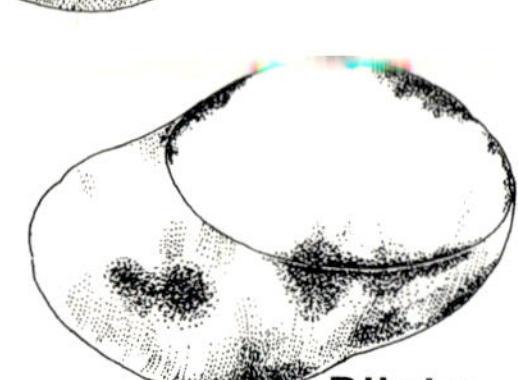

Blight Destructive disease affecting potatoes, chiefly maincrops, and tomatoes. Potato tops become blotched with brown and yellow and die off. The fungal sores affect the tubers, which decay. The disease is active in warm, wet weather and if leaf discoloration is seen at such times the crop should be sprayed with Bordeaux Mixture or a proprietary equivalent as a pretion.

Carrots

Carrot fly. Avoid attracting the fly when thinning. (See Thinning.) Disguise the carrot scent by sprinkling naphthalene beside the rows.

Wireworms, slugs and leather jackets. If damage has been serious apply a soil pesticide the following year. Leather jackets, the larvae of the crane fly, are only an occasional hazard. Wireworms (see Potatoes, above) not only bore holes in roots but attack all young plants below ground. Dig up any suddenly wilting seedling and look for the pest in the soil.

Onions

The keeping quality of bulbs grown from sets may be affected by diseases such as white rot. Buy only certified heat-treated sets. Onion fly operates in the same way as carrot fly and the same precautions should be taken.

Parsnips

The parsnip is virtually pest-free and the only disease is parsnip canker, which is a nuisance on some soils. Grow the variety Avonresister where it occurs.

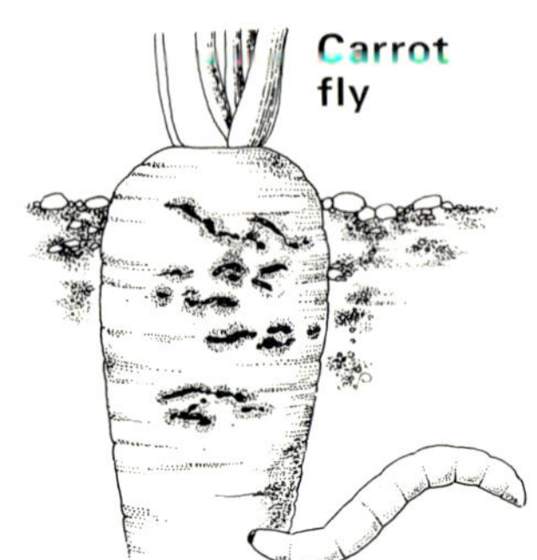

Turnips and swedes

The seedlings of both are attacked by flea beetle, as are seedling brassicas and radishes. The beetle is most active in dry weather, puncturing and eventually des-

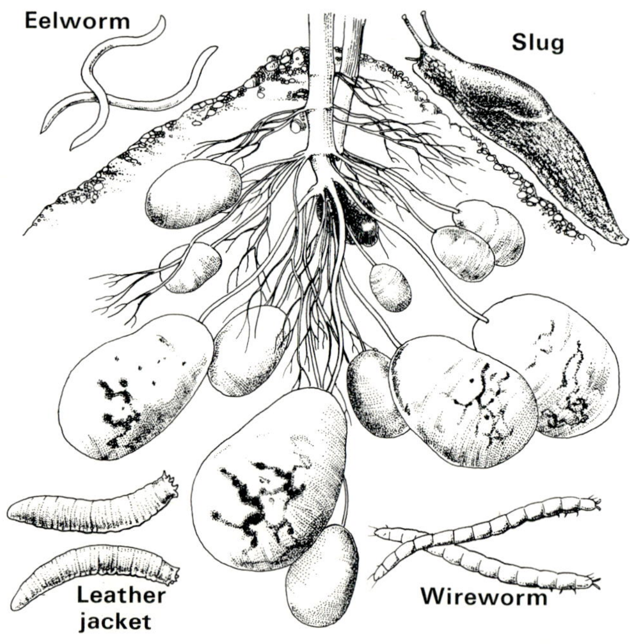

troying the seed leaves. The seedling is safe when it develops its first true leaves. Dust repeatedly with derris and water the seedlings to keep them growing.

BRASSICA CROPS

All brassicas are affected by the following:

Caterpillars of the cabbage white butterfly. These lay their eggs on the undersides of leaves and several broods may hatch in the summer, stripping the foliage. Hand-pick the caterpillars if there are not many plants and spray with a garden aerosol.

Cabbage aphids. Grey patches of aphids, spread into sprouts and cabbage hearts and ruin the crop if not checked. Spray with malathion before the colonies are established in inaccessible places.

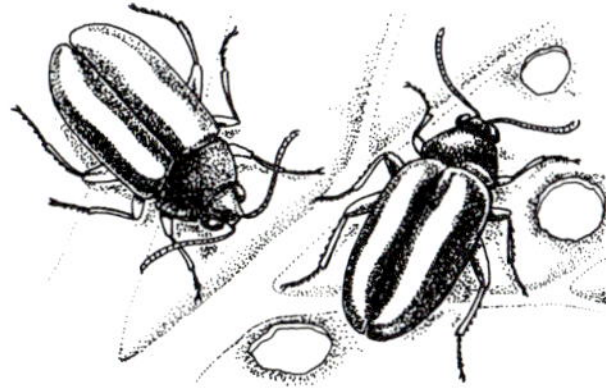

Flea beetle

Club root is the one common disease of brassicas, also affecting swedes and turnips with poor growth and deformed and swollen roots. Lime affected ground heavily, applying 0.5kg per sq m and a light dressing the following year. Rotate brassica crops regularly and as a precaution dip the roots of young brassicas in a thin paste of 4 per cent Calomel dust before planting out.

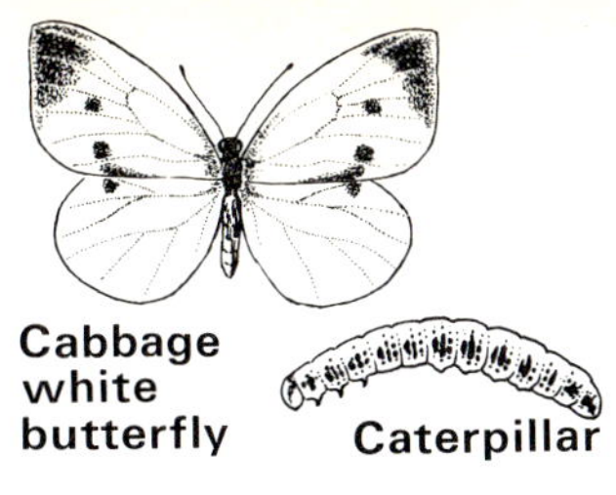

Cabbage white butterfly **Caterpillar**

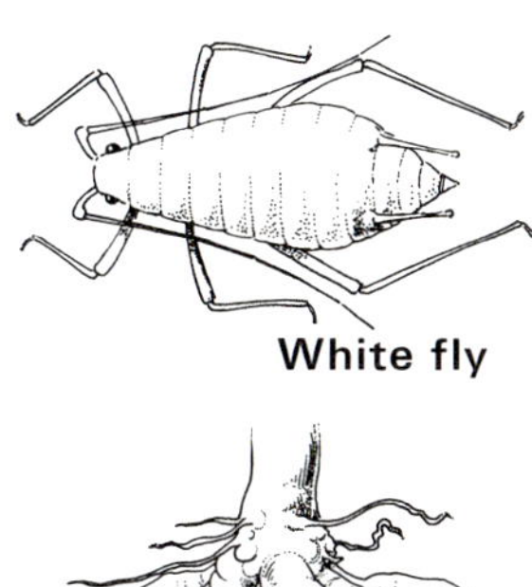

White fly

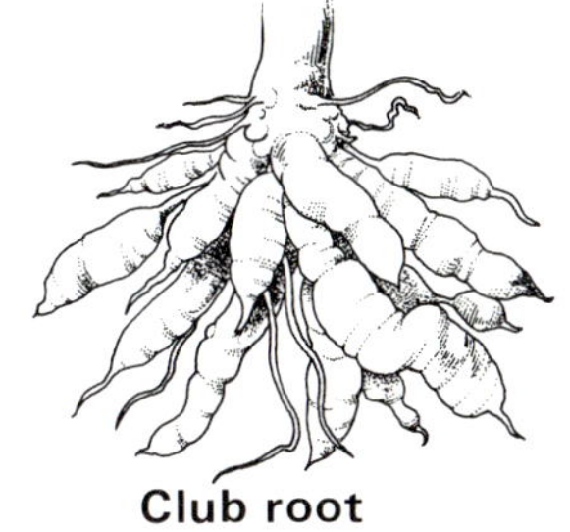

Club root

Cauliflowers

In addition to the usual run of brassica troubles cauliflowers are a prime target for the cabbage root fly, which lays its eggs at the foot of the young plant so that its larvae can feed on the roots. The plant wilts and collapses. Incorporate a soil pesticide or 4 per cent Calomel dust on the soil around each plant at planting time. Dig up affected plants with soil and grubs and burn them.

PEAS AND BEANS

Garden peas

Apart from birds, which attack the seedlings, the only serious pest is the pea moth, whose larvae are the maggots found in the pods. Early varieties are seldom affected and the trouble is usually worse in dry seasons. As a preventative, spray the flowers with a garden insecticide when they first open and repeat ten days later. Spraying the pods is useless.

Runner and broad beans

Both are liable to attack by black aphids (blackfly or colliers) though the broad bean suffers most. The aphids start in the growing point of the plant and, as they reproduce by both egg-laying and the production of live young, multiply very rapidly. Pick out the growing points when a reasonable amount of bloom has set and this will nip the aphid colonies in the bud and at the same time hasten the development of the pods. Follow it up by spraying any aphids found elsewhere.

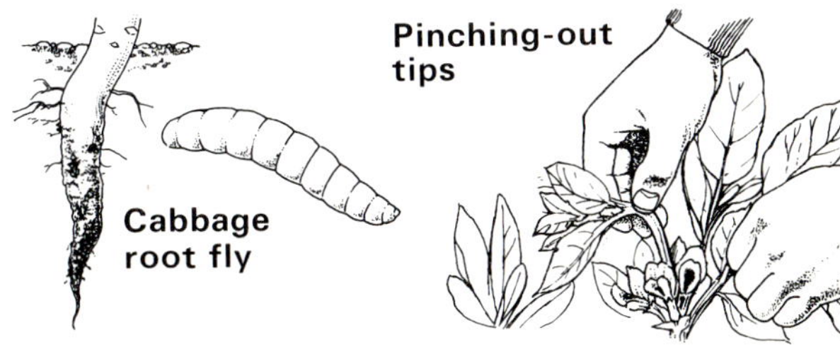

Cabbage root fly

Pinching-out tips

Blackfly on runners appear first in the tips of the flower spikes. Keep a close watch and spray before it has a chance to spread.

SALAD CROPS

Tomatoes

Few insect pests except for white fly on greenhouse crops which lives on the underside of leaves and is related to the aphids. Leaves and fruit become black and sticky. Spray with garden aerosol *repeatedly* and fumigate with greenhouse fumigant if this fails.

Blossom-end rot is caused by plants drying out when the fruits are swelling, a brown patch appearing during ripening. Fruit-splitting is also caused by failure to keep the plants uniformly moist.

Blotchy ripening and greenback are due to very high temperatures and potash deficiency. Ventilate freely, shade in the hottest weather, and use a high-potash liquid feed. Grow varieties resistant to greenback.

White fly and blossom-end rot

Outdoor crops are susceptible to potato blight. Grow as far from potatoes as possible and under blight conditions use a protective spray on both.

FRUIT: TOP FRUIT

Apples

Two pests are responsible for maggots in fruit. One is the codling moth, which lays eggs on the fruitlets in early summer. The grubs burrow into the apples, emerge two months later and spend the winter as cocoons under the bark. Spray with lindane

Apple saw fly

Codling moth

when the petals fall and again ten days later.

The apple sawfly has a similar life-history, but the grub emerges from the fallen apple and pupates in the soil. Spray at petal-fall with derris, pick apples with holes in them from mid-summer onwards, and collect and destroy unusable windfalls promptly. Cultivate the soil under the trees in winter to disturb the pupae. Use grease bands or traps of sacking or corrugated paper round trunk and branches.

Peaches and nectarines

Leaf blister is the commonest trouble. Red patches appear on affected leaves, developing into large blisters. The leaves fall and the disease increases yearly, jeopardizing the crop. Collect and burn fallen leaves and spray the tree in midwinter, just before bud burst with liquid copper fungicide.

Plums

Aphid infestation can be very severe, the pest building up on a tree year after

Leaf curl

Aphids

year. New growth, fruit, and even the ground under the tree are covered with a sticky black secretion. Spray very thoroughly with a tar oil wash in winter to kill the

Silver leaf

eggs and with a contact insecticide just before the blossom opens to finish off any live insects.

Silver leaf disease causes progressive dieback of branches, the foliage turning a mildewed silvery colour and a dark stain appearing in the wood. Cut back the branch to clean wood 15cm beyond the stain and cover the wound with bitumin paint. This, and all other pruning should be done in summer.

Big bud

SOFT FRUIT

Blackcurrants

The gall mite feeds on the inside of flower buds, producing the swollen 'big bud' which gives the condition its name. Pick off and destroy these big buds. Spray

Magpie moth

with lime sulphur when the leaves are 3cm across.

Buy only certified stock as a precaution against reversion, which is a virus disease, not a genetic failure.

Gooseberries

Generally trouble-free, but caterpillars of the gooseberry sawfly and the magpie moth can soon defoliate bushes in late spring. Keep a careful watch, hand-pick the caterpillars, and spray

or dust with derris insecticide.

Raspberry beetle

Raspberries

The small maggots found in the fruit are the larvae of the raspberry beetle. It is not a universal pest and in many gardens seems never to occur at all. Control by thoroughly spraying with derris in the late evening when the blossom is fully open.

Strawberries

In a wet season an attack of grey mould or botrytis can be devastating. The berries rot near the stalk, becoming a furry mass of mould and infecting all those nearby. As a preventive, spray the flowers soon after opening with benamyl (Benlate).

Grey mould

Sowing and planting chart

ROOT CROPS	Time to germination (days)	When to sow	Spacing in row
Artichokes (Jerusalem)	tubers	Feb–March	30cm
Beetroot	10–17	April–July	20cm
Carrots	10–21	April–July	7·5–10cm
Leeks	21	March–April	15–22cm
Onions	21	March	15cm
Parsnips	21–28	March	10–15cm
Potatoes (Maincrop)	seed tubers	April–May	37·5cm
Swedes	5–10	April–June	22·5cm
Turnips	5–14	March–June	15–22·5cm
BRASSICA CROPS			
Brussels sprouts	10–14	March	45–60cm
Cabbage Autumn Summer Spring Winter	7–14 (Autumn, Summer) 6–10 (Spring, Winter)	Jan–Feb (under glass) (Autumn, Summer) July–Aug May	45cm 37·5cm 22·5cm 45cm
Calabrese	10–14	April	45cm
Cauliflower Winter Summer Autumn	6–10 7–14 (Summer, Autumn)	April–May February April	60cm 45cm 60cm
Sprouting broccoli	7–14	April–May	45cm
PEAS AND BEANS			
Broad beans	14–24	Feb–April	15cm
Dwarf beans	14–21	April–May	10cm
Runner beans	14–21	May	15cm one row
Garden peas	10–17	Autumn, Spring, early Summer	2cm
Asparagus peas	10–14	early Spring	7cm (45cm under glass)

Planting depth	Space between rows	Season of use	Sowing to harvest (months)	Packeted seed life
10cm	1m	Aut–Spring	7	(tubers)
2cm	30cm	June–Feb	2	(roots stored)
2cm	30cm	June onwards	2½–3	1 year
15cm	45cm	Oct–March	8	3 years
1·5cm	30cm	from July	4	buy new yearly
2·5cm	37·5cm	Oct–April	7	1 season only
12·5cm	67·5cm	Aug–June	5	(tubers)
1·5cm	45cm	Oct–April	6	several years
1·5cm	30cm	June–late Aut	3	several years
2cm (seed)	60cm for plants	Sept–March	6	several years
2cm (seed)	60cm 45cm 45cm 60cm	June–Nov	4	2–4 years
2cm (seed)	60cm	Aug–Nov	4	2–4 years
2cm (seed)	60cm 45cm 60cm	Nov–May June–July Aug–Nov	7 4	3–4 years
2cm (seed)	60cm	Feb–May	10	3 years
5cm	60–75cm	June–Aug	3–4	2 years
3cm	60cm	June–Aug	3	2 years
5cm	30cm	July–Oct	3–3½	2 years
5–7cm	60cm	June–Sept	3–3½	2 years
1cm		July	4	2 years

Sowing and planting chart

SALAD CROPS	Time to germination (days)	When to sow	Spacing in row
Celery	14–21	March	22cm for self-blanching
Chicory	12–14	early Summer	15cm
Cucumbers Indoor Outdoor	5–7 7–10	May May (under glass)	1·2m 1·2m
Lettuce	7–14	March–July	22–30cm
Radish	5–8	March–Sept	2cm
Salad onions	21	March–June	15cm
Tomatoes Indoor Outdoor	10	March April	45cm { tall 45cm bush 60cm
MISCELLANEOUS CROPS			
Artichokes (Globe)	buy plants	April	1m
Asparagus	buy 2-year-old plants	April	30cm
Aubergines	18–25	March	45cm
Celeriac	10–14	March	30cm
Marrows and Courgettes	7–10	May	75cm (for pumpkins and trailing marrows 1·2m)
Mushrooms	See page 80 for information		
Seakale beet	10–14	late April	30cm
Spinach	7–12	March–July	22cm
Sweetcorn	10–14	May	45cm
Squashes	6–10	May	1m

Planting depth	Space between rows	Season of use	Sowing to harvest (months)	Packeted Seed life
1–2cm	22cm	Aut–Winter	5	2–3 years
1–2cm	45cm	Winter	5	2–3 years
1·5cm		July–Oct	2	several years
2cm	30cm	June–Oct	3	2 years
2cm	15cm	April–Oct	1	3–4 years
1·5cm	25cm	May–Oct	3	1 season only
1–2cm		July–Nov Aug–Oct	4	2 years
(plants)	1m	July–Sept	3	
22cm	1m	April–June	13	
2cm		Aug–Sept	5	1 year
bulb at base of seedling resting on earth	45cm	Aut–Spring	7	2–3 years
2cm		July–Sept (Oct–Jan ripened from store)	2	unreliable but up to several years
See page 80 for information				
2·5cm	35cm	late Sum–Aut	4	2 years
2·5cm	35cm	Sept–May	4	2 years
2·5cm	45cm	July–Oct	3–4	2 years. Buy fresh
2cm		July–Sept	3–5	1 year

Planting and pruning chart

SOFT FRUIT	When to plant	Season of use	Planting to harvest
Blackberries	Autumn	July–October	21 months
Blackcurrants	October–March	July–September	18 months
Gooseberries	Autumn	May–July	18 months
Hybrid berries and Loganberries	October–March	July–August	20 months
Raspberries	See page 83 for information		
Red and White Currants	Autumn–early Spring	July	18 months
Strawberries	See page 83 for information		
TOP FRUIT			
Apples	November–March	August–April	2 years
Cherries	Autumn	July–September	4 years
Grapes	See page 84 for information		
Peaches and Nectarines	Autumn	July–September	3 years
Pears	Autumn	August–February	2 years
Plums, Gages and Damsons	Autumn	July–October	2–3 years

	When to prune	Cultivation	Suitability for freezing
	after planting and fruiting	mulch in Spring	1 year
	November–December	mulch in Spring	1 year
	regularly	beware extra growth	whole and uncooked or purée 1 year
	after planting and fruiting	needs mulching and support	1 year. Very good for jam
	See page 83 for information		
	November–December	mulch in late Spring	1 year or make redcurrant jelly
	See page 83 for information		
	Winter or mid–Summer	do not allow young trees to crop heavily	1 year for pies or as purée
	regularly	keep moist and weed-free	1 year. Morello a good freezer
	See page 84 for information		
	Mid-summer and autumn	thin out fruits	1 year. Freeze in syrup
	regularly	protect against frost	lose quality 1 year in syrup
	summer	beware of silver leaf disease and aphids	reasonably good for 1 year

THE SEASONS

The months in brackets are for gardeners in the southern hemisphere only.

Early spring
March
(September)
Mid-spring
April
(October)
Late spring
May
(November)
Early summer
June
(December)
Mid-summer
July
(January)
Late summer
August
(February)
Early autumn
September
(March)
Mid-autumn
October
(April)
Late autumn
November
(May)
Early winter
January
(July)
Late winter
February
(August)

Growing guide

ROOT CROPS: ARTICHOKES, JERUSALEM

Edible tuber, not universally popular with cooks or consumers because of irregular shape and earthy flavour. Nutritious, pest- and disease-free and very hardy. Grows anywhere, but well cultivated soil in good heart produces tubers of better shape and quality. Difficult to eradicate once planted as small and broken tubers come up again.

The stems are about 2m tall and serve as a quick-growing screen if kept in place with a few posts and strands of wire. In the autumn they are cut down, leaving about 15cm to mark the position of the row. The tubers are dug as required. Apart from routine weeding while the plants are small little attention is needed during the growing period.

Varieties There are no distinct varieties. If tubers for planting are not obtainable from the seedsman use those sold by the greengrocer for cooking.

BEETROOT

A slightly tender crop. Spring sowing should not be made early unless cloched. Seedlings are easily damaged by frost and any spell of cold weather may cause bolting later.

The ideal soil is one with plenty of humus to retain moisture but without fresh manure. Select ground manured for a previous crop and apply a light dressing of compound fertilizer before sowing. A successional summer sowing to provide small roots for pulling in autumn should follow early peas or broad beans. The drill for this sowing should be watered and the watering continued until the seedlings are established.

Thin best early, taking care to single the seedlings where they have come up in clusters.

Varieties For early sowing: Boltardy, Avon-early, Early Bunch. Later sowing and for storage: Cylindra, Crimson Globe.

CARROTS

One of the most important root crops for immediate use, freezing while young and storing naturally when mature. The best yields are obtained on light or medium soils but the short or stump-rooted varieties do quite well on heavy soils if properly cultivated. Use no fresh organic manure but rake in a pre-sowing dressing of 60g per sq m of a compound fertilizer.

Make three sowings if space permits. A small quick-growing variety in early spring, a larger type for storing in late spring, and an early variety in mid-summer to provide small roots for immediate use and freezing in the autumn. This is a useful successional crop to follow early potatoes. Carrots respond to effective weed control, timely thinning and regular watering in dry weather. Overcrowding gives the roots no chance to swell and an irregular water supply causes splitting.

Varieties For early and late sowings: Amsterdam Forcing, Early Nantes, Chantenay. Maincrop: New Red Intermediate, James' Intermediate. All seasons and on all soils: Early Scarlet Horn.

LEEKS

A hardy winter vegetable. Sow in the seed-bed in spring, using pelleted seed or thinning early and drastically so that the seedlings stand at least 5cm apart in the rows.

Dig in manure or compost when preparing the soil and

lightly fork in a dressing of fertilizer at the usual rate before planting. Leeks are unlike other root crops and respond to heavy manuring with improved quality as well as yield.

Plant as described on p.350. Water freely in dry weather and give fortnightly feed of liquid fertilizer if growth is slow. Always lift leeks with a fork.

Varieties For autumn use: Early Market. For winter use: The Lyon, Marble Pillar, Musselburgh.

ONIONS

Onions are grown from either seed or sets. Seed may be sown in spring or autumn, but spring sowing is more reliable in most districts. Sets are specially treated small onions grown crowded together the previous year. When planted in spring they resume their growth. Shallots, milder flavoured than onions, are planted like sets.

Onions require an open, sunny situation and a soil deeply dug in winter after being manured for a previous crop. Rake the surface to the finest possible tilth, incorporating 30g per sq m of a compound fertilizer.

Sow thinly and cover the seed lightly. Do not allow the seedlings to become overcrowded to prolong the supply of thinnings for salads, thin the bulb onions like other crops and sow salad onions separately.

Plant sets with a trowel with only the neck protruding. Snip off dead skin before planting; earth-worms get hold of it and drag the set out of the ground.

Varieties Seed: Ailsa Craig, Bedfordshire Champion, Red Globe, James' Long Keeping, Giant Zittau. Sets: Stuttgarter, Giant Fen Globe.

PARSNIPS

One of the hardiest root crops. Soil requires no organic manure, only a light pre-sowing dressing of a compound fertilizer; fresh manure causes forked and generally malformed roots. Deep and thorough digging is essential, especially if long varieties are being grown. It has long been the practice, when growing for exhibition, to make holes with a crowbar, fill them with prepared soil, and establish one plant in each.

Thin early and in stages. The thinnings, like those of swedes are of no culinary use, parsnips gain their full flavour only with the onset of winter.

Varieties For deep soils: The Student, Hollow Crown. For shallow soils and where parsnip canker has occurred: Avonresister.

POTATOES

The most important root crop, a staple carbohydrate food and major source of vitamin C.

Soil for potatoes should be open and friable, containing plenty of humus but not necessarily heavily manured. A combination of peat and 60g per m of a compound fertilizer is satisfactory.

Plant earlies some three weeks before the last probable date for spring frost. Plant maincrops a week or two later.

Sprout the seed tubers in a light, frost-free place. Plant in a trench, taking care not to damage the shoots. Cover each tuber with a generous double handful of peat. Scatter the fertilizer over the soil taken from the trench and rake the soil back over the tubers, mixing the fertilizer with it. Fork lightly between the rows, leaving all the soil loose.

When the plants emerge, draw soil over them if night frost threatens. When they are about 20cm high earth them up more fully, pulling the soil from both sides with the draw hoe so that the row becomes a ridge from which only the tips of the plants protrude. Again fork between the rows, leaving the soil fit for further earthing up if necessary.

Hoe and hand weed until the tops meet in the rows. Water well in dry spells.

Varieties Earlies: Arran Pilot, Home Guard, Epicure, Sharpe's Express, Foremost. For dry conditions: Home Guard. For quality: Foremost. For quick recovery after frost: Epicure. Maincrops: Majestic, Maris Piper, Pentland crown, Desiree, King Edward, Golden Wonder.

SWEDES

An excellent winter vegetable and a good keeper.

Soil requirements, sowing and cultivation are the same as for turnips. The main difference is in timing. Swedes are not pulled during the summer and are only ready to eat when properly mature in the autumn. They are therefore not sown early but in late spring or summer. The later sowings, about mid-summer, give best results provided the seedlings are given a good start by watering if necessary and are protected from flea beetle. The most rapid growth is made in early autumn.

Varieties Purple Top, Western Perfection, Best of All.

TURNIPS

A hardy crop, but even so is best not sown too early in spring as this encourages bolting. Soil should be in good heart, not freshly manured, but with a 100g per sq m dressing of a compound fertilizer to promote rapid growth. Complaints of stringiness and a 'strong' flavour in turnips are usually due to slow growth on poor soils.

Successional sowings may be made up to mid-summer. It is a good idea to make a final sowing broadcast. Mark out a strip 60 cm wide, rake it to a level tilth and remove weeds. Scatter the seed over it very thinly and either rake it in or cover lightly with fine soil. Water if necessary until germination in about five days time. Large numbers of small roots may be pulled in a normal winter and the strip may eventually be cloched to provide early turnip tops for spring greens.

Varieties For early sowing: Early Snowball, Tokyo Cross. Later sowing and storage: White Milan, Golden Ball. Wintering outdoors: Green Top Stone.

BRASSICA CROPS: BRUSSELS SPROUTS

A main standby among winter greens, cropping from mid-autumn to early spring if early and late varieties are grown. This hardy crop survives prolonged frost, but needs some shelter from strong winds.

Heavy soil is preferred to light and it should be very firm and in good heart. Winter digging and manuring should be finished early to give the soil time to settle. If there is any suspicion of soil acidity apply garden lime at 180g per sq m after digging. Rake in 80g per sq m of a compound fertilizer just before planting.

Sprouts appreciate a long growing season. Plants may be raised in the greenhouse and planted out in spring, or seed may be sown in the outdoor seed-bed in early spring and the plants moved to the prepared site in early summer.

It is not a good idea to plant sprouts in succession to early potatoes. This often entails delay, and it is better to have a site ready and to move the plants from the seed-bed as soon as they are fit. The prepared ground need not lie idle but may be used for a catch crop of quick-growing lettuce such as Tom Thumb. Sow it in early spring and interplant with the sprouts when they are ready.

Varieties Early: Peer Gynt, Cambridge No. 1, Bedford Fillbasket. For freezing: Roodnerf. For light soils: Siltrex. Late: Cambridge No. 5.

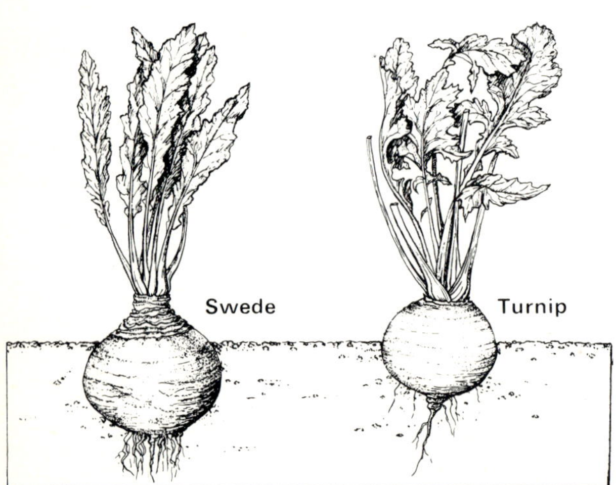

CABBAGES, AUTUMN AND WINTER

A useful crop which includes the very hardy savoys and the Dutch white types which may be cut and stored in hard weather.

The situation should be open and sunny, well away from the drip of overhanging trees, and this applies to all overwintered crops. The ground should be deeply dug, and the sub-soil broken up if it is at all prone to waterlogging. Lime after digging if necessary.

Sow in the seed-bed in late spring, thinning drastically or using well-spaced pelleted seeds to obtain stocky plants. Planting out may have to be done in hot weather and the transplants must be watered until well established. Later, if they seem to be slow growing they may be top dressed with compound fertilizer, 60g per 1m of row, hoed and watered in. This must be done before the end of summer so as not to promote late soft growth.

Varieties Autumn maturing: Winningstadt, Autumn Supreme. Winter maturing: January King, Christmas Drumhead, Ice Queen, Best of All, Rearguard. For cutting and storing: Winter White.

CABBAGES, SPRING AND SUMMER

Spring cabbages are sown in late summer, transplanted in autumn and harvested in late spring and early summer. They need a good, well-drained but not over-rich soil and can follow runner beans or maincrop potatoes with little preparation.

If you have a surplus of plants space them at only half the recommended distance and use every other one for springs when sufficiently leafy, leaving the rest to heart up. If growth is slow, top dress with sulphate of ammonia, 30g per 1m of row.

Summer cabbages are sown under glass for the early summer crop and planted out when hardened off. They are not damaged by light spring frosts. Soil should be well dug and manured in the winter and dressed with 80g per sq m of a compound fertilizer before planting.

Varieties Spring (sow in late summer): Harbinger, April, Flower of Spring, Ellams Early. Summer (sow in spring): Early: Velocity, Greyhound, Hispi. Later: Primo, Stonehead, Golden Acre. Red or pickling: Ruby Ball.

CALABRESE

A green sprouting broccoli from the Calabria region of Italy. Unlike the white and purple forms it is not winter-hardy and is sown in spring for use in late summer and autumn before the frosts come. It is increasingly popular and freezes well.

For good yield and quality calabrese requires generous treatment. Dig and manure the ground in winter and rake in the usual dressing of fertilizer before planting. If treated as a successional crop it should follow broad beans or early peas. Occasional feeds of liquid fertilizer help towards the necessary quick growth.

Sow in the seed-bed in late spring and plant out when about 10cm high. If you are late with this sowing, sow where plants are to grow and thin out. This may be done up to mid-summer.

Varieties Early: Express Corona. Autumn: Atlantic, Autumn Spear, Green Comet. The last has a large central head but fewer side shoots than other varieties.

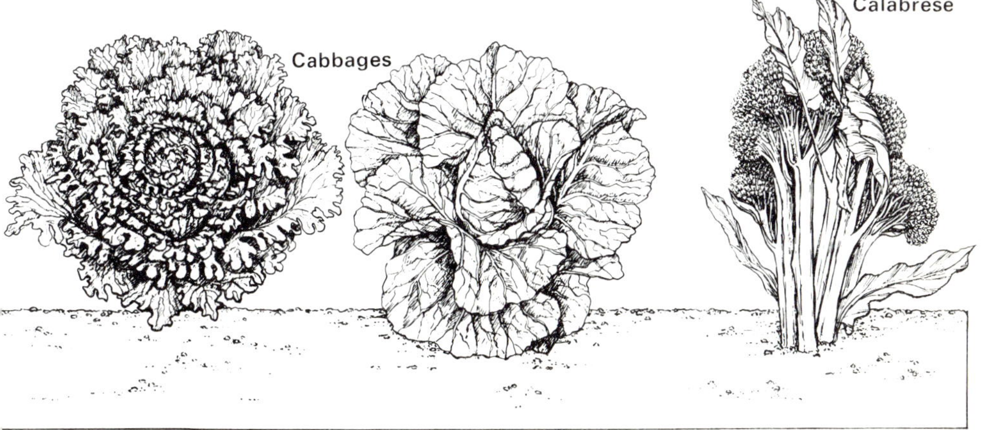

CAULIFLOWERS, SUMMER AND AUTUMN

Early summer cauliflowers are raised under glass or bought from the nurseryman for planting as soon as the danger of severe spring frosts is over. Late summer and autumn varieties are sown in the outdoor seed-bed and transplanted when ready.

Cauliflowers need rather more fussing than most brassicas, and the small early varieties are well worth it. Maintain uninterrupted growth, raising the seedlings singly in peat pots for trouble-free planting. Any serious check may cause the plants to 'button' or form small premature curds.

Soil should be well manured and 80g per sq m of a compound fertilizer raked in before planting. Keep well watered in dry weather.

Varieties Early summer: Snowball, Snow King, Classic. Mid-season: Dominant, All the Year Round. Autumn: Kangaroo, Barrier Reef, Bondi. The last three are fine, compact Australian introductions.

CAULIFLOWERS, WINTER

Hardy. Sown in the seed-bed in late spring, planted out in summer, and maturing from late autumn onwards according to variety.

Soil should be good but not too rich in nitrogen or growth will be soft and susceptible to frost damage. Use a compound fertilizer containing potash, which increases frost resistance, rather than a straight nitrogenous one. Apply it either before planting or as a top dressing well before autumn. The site should be open, sunny and well drained.

Varieties Late autumn: Veitch's Self-protecting. Winter and spring: St George, Reading Giant. Late spring: Late Queen, June Market.

SPROUTING BROCCOLI

The flowering shoots with their unopened buds are picked from late winter to early summer, according to variety and season. Easy to grow and popular. Freezes well.

Sow in the seed-bed in late spring and plant out when 10cm high. If this sowing is missed, sow where it is to grow and thin to final distance. This may be a successional sowing and can be made as late as mid-summer.

Soil, like that for winter cauliflowers, should be good but not over manured. The site should be sunny with, if possible, some protection from freezing winds.

Varieties Two distinct types, white and purple. The purple, which cooks to an attractive deep green, is generally preferred. There is a subdivision into early and late, but varietal names like Extra Early or Early Winter need not be taken too seriously. The weather is all important.

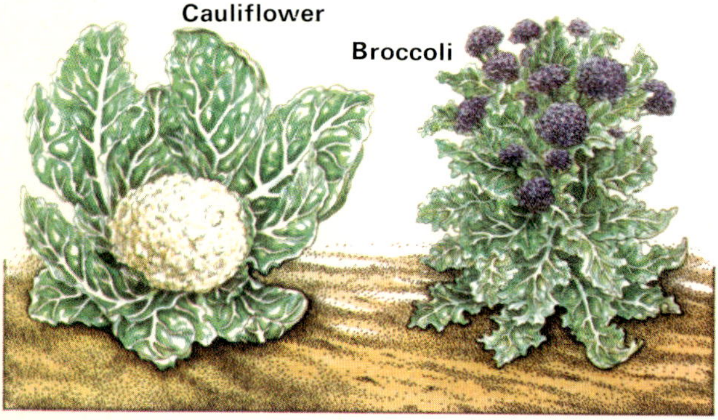

Cauliflower

Broccoli

PEAS AND BEANS: BROAD BEANS

Earliest crops are produced by a mid-autumn sowing. A hardy Longpod variety will survive an average winter unprotected and a fairly severe one if cloched. Longpods are also sown very early in spring, followed a few weeks later by the Windsor varieties, regarded as slightly less hardy and of better quality.

Organic manures are unnecessary on heavy or medium soils. On light land manure or compost dug in during the winter is valuable for its moisture-holding properties. A dressing of 160g per sq m of garden lime should be applied after digging if the soil is at all acid and a light pre-sowing dose of a compound fertilizer gives the crop a good start.

Sow in a wide drill made with the full blade of the draw hoe, 2cm deeper for the late spring and autumn sowings than for the spring ones. Space the seeds in a double staggered row. Pinch out the tops when a reasonable crop has set.

Varieties For autumn sowing: Claudia Aquadulce (Giant Seville); this variety is useless for spring sowing. Longpods for autumn or early spring: Dreadnought, Exhibition Longpod, Longfellow, Masterpiece. Windsors: White Windsor, Imperial Green Windsor. Dwarf types for the small garden: The Sutton, The Midget.

DWARF BEANS

Dwarf French beans are widely grown. The climbing French bean is less well known, climbing to a height of 1.25m. It crops more heavily than the dwarf and except for supporting canes or net requires the same treatment. A good choice for the small garden.

The crop is tender and must not be sown in the open while there is a risk of frost or before the soil has warmed up. Cloche sowings may be made three weeks earlier, forwarding the first picking by at least a month. Put the cloches in position a week before sowing, use a dwarf variety and decloche when the plants reach the glass, by which time they should be almost in bloom.

A sunny, sheltered position and a lightish soil are ideal. Heavy soils are improved by digging in some well rotted manure or compost. Rake in 80g per sq m of a compound fertilizer with a good potash content before sowing.

Sow in a double staggered row in a wide drill, with extra seeds for making up.

For climbing varieties place supports along the centre of the row or, better still, on both sides of it. Dwarf varieties flop badly when in full bearing; earth up the stems and support the pod clusters. Water freely in dry weather. Pick regularly.

Varieties For early and cloche work: Earligreen, Tendergreen. Both recommended for freezing. For heavy yield: The Prince, Masterpiece. For cold districts: Glamis. For use green or dried as haricots: Chevrier Vert, Comtesse de Chamborde. Climbing: Romano, Purple Podded. Very high quality stringless: Kinghorn Waxpod, Sprite.

RUNNER BEANS

Valuable crop giving a high return on space if allowed to climb to a reasonable height.

The runner bean is tender, easily destroyed by frost and unlikely to germinate in cold ground. Cloche sowings may be given a three weeks start on those in the open, but must be uncovered as soon as they touch the cloche or they will attach themselves to any projection. Plants may also be started in the greenhouse or frame, seeds being spaced 5cm apart and 3cm deep in potting compost and the plants set out after hardening off just before they start to 'run'.

If the plants are to be grown on a wigwam of poles put this in position and sow a few seeds or put in a plant at the foot of each pole. Single or double rows may be sown and either staked when the plants are up or dwarfed by pinching back.

Runners need plenty of food and water. Dig thoroughly in winter, working in any available compost or manure, apply a pre-sowing dressing of a compound fertilizer and mulch the growing crop with compost or peat.

Varieties For earliest crop: Kelvedon Marvel, Scarlet Emperor. For quality and length of pod: Streamline, Prizewinner, Enorma. White flowered and seeded: White Achievement, White Wonder. Seeds of the last named may be dried and used as butter beans. Hammonds Dwarf Scarlet grows a little larger than dwarf French varieties, its pods are a fair size but the crop is not large.

◀ Dwarf beans ready for harvesting.

▼ The Scarlet Emperor variety of runner bean.

GARDEN PEAS

Peas are among the most valuable of summer crops for immediate use or for freezing. Peas should be closely picked while young giving the plants a greater incentive to produce more.

Sowings of early varieties are made in late winter under cloches and in early spring in the open. These are followed at three-weekly intervals by second earlies and maincrops, with a final sowing of first earlies about mid-summer. An autumn sowing under cloches succeeds in an average winter and yields a very early crop.

Soil for peas should be in good heart and not deficient in lime. Apply a 80g per sq m dressing of fertilizer before sowing. Water well if dry weather sets in when the pods are forming.

Varieties For autumn sowing: Meteor, Sleaford Phoenix. Spring sowing under cloche: the above, also Histon Mini, Feltham First. Early sowing in the open: any of the above, also Kelvedon Wonder, Pioneer, Hurst Beagle. Maincrops: Early Onward, Onward, Greenshaft. Final sowing: Kelvedon Wonder, Hurst Beagle. Edible podded (sugar peas or mangetouts): Dwarf Sweetgreen, Carouby de Maussane. The last is a tall variety, all the others recommended are dwarfs.

ASPARAGUS PEAS

The asparagus pea is not a true pea and is more allied to the lotus. It is bushy rather than climbing, half-hardy, and bears masses of pinkish flowers followed by small oblong pods with an asparagus flavour. The total weight of crop is not large but if the little pods are kept closely picked and no seeds allowed to form the plants remain productive for quite a time.

Sow under glass in early spring, two or three seeds to a small peat pot filled with potting compost. Reduce the seedlings to one per pot, grow on close to the glass and plant out 20cm apart when risk of frost is over.

No great soil preparation is needed—or possible, if the plants are to be grouped in a flower border. Fork in a little organic manure or compost well in advance of planting, plus a sprinkle of fertilizer at planting time.

Varieties No distinct varieties. Listed as Asparagus Pea, usually in the Garden Pea section of the catalogue.

SALAD CROPS: CELERY

Blanching celery is grown in a trench, earthed up and used in late autumn and winter. Self-blanching types are grown on the flat, are not earthed up and are used in summer and early autumn before really cold weather sets in. Both types are sown under glass in early spring and planted out in summer. Buy plants if only a few are needed, but be sure which type you are getting.

Blanching celery Take out a trench one spit deep and 30cm wide some weeks before planting time. Throw the soil into a flat-topped ridge and grow a quick-maturing salad crop on it. Dig manure or compost into the bottom of the trench. Plant a single row down the centre and keep well watered. In late summer gather the stems of each plant together and tie loosely near the top. Earth up with soil from the ridge in stages at intervals of three weeks, packing it carefully round the plants. Continue until a new ridge is formed with only tufts of leaves visible at the top.

Self-blanching celery Prepare the ground by digging in organic manure plus an 80g per sq m dose of a compound

Garden peas

Asparagus peas

Celery

fertilizer before planting to ensure quick growth. Plant in a block, with rows and plants equidistant at 20cm, so that the plants grow in a compact mass and shade one another. Water generously.
Varieties Blanching: Giant White, Giant Pink, White Ice. Self-blanching: Avon Pearl, Golden Self-blanching, Greensnap, American Green.

CHICORY
Sow seed in early summer on ground in good heart and not acid. Thin the seedlings in stages, always giving them plenty of room. Keep well watered and give an occasional liquid feed.

In late autumn, when the tops die down, start lifting the roots for forcing. Remove the dead tops, taking care not to injure the crowns. Place a number of roots upright in a pot or box and fill it to the tops of the roots with potting compost. Keep in a moderately warm place in complete darkness and prevent the compost drying out.

The new, blanched growth is cut before the leaves begin to unfold, the roots discarded and a new batch brought in.
Varieties The Brussels Chicory, Witloof, is generally grown. There is a pink variety called Red Verona and a new one called Sugar Loaf.

CUCUMBERS, INDOOR
The greenhouse cucumber likes a temperature not much below 15°C. It should not be sown or planted until early summer in the cold-house, but given the right conditions growth is very rapid. One properly trained cucumber requires as much space as three tomato plants.

Sow seeds in peat pots and plant at the two- to four-leaf stage, or order in advance from a nursery.

Plant on mounds of soil or potting compost 1.25m apart on the border or in boxes or large pots on the staging. Allow a pailful of the growing medium to each plant.

Plant the cucumbers on the shadiest side of the house. Provide each with a vertical cane and horizontal wires 30cm apart. Train the main stem up the cane and laterals along the wires. Stop fruiting shoots two leaves beyond the fruit.

Keep well watered but avoid wetting the stem at ground level, which may cause stem rot. Growing on a mound ensures more effective drainage. As fruit is spoiled by pollination, pick off male blooms or grow all-female types.
Varieties For easy cultivation: Conqueror. For large fruit: Telegraph Improved. For exceptional quality: Sigmadew. All female types: Femina, Femspot, Topsy.

CUCUMBERS, OUTDOOR
Prepare sites, one for each plant, in a sunny, sheltered position. Take out a hole one spit deep, mix the soil with well rotted manure or compost, and replace it in the hole, shaping it into a low mound.

Only a few plants are needed for the average family. Buy them or raise them under glass, sowing three seeds to a small peat pot filled with potting compost, reducing to one seedling, and hardening off before planting out. Alternatively, sow three seeds on the top of each mound and reduce to one plant.

Sow or plant outdoors only when there is no risk of frost. Avoid root disturbance when planting. Protect from slugs with metaldehyde pellets.

When the plant has six leaves nip out the growing point and laterals will develop. They may be trained up supports or left on the ground, tiles or pieces of polythene being placed under the fruits. Leave the male blooms on as fertilization is necessary.

Water frequently round and not over the plant, keeping the stem dry. Give a fortnightly liquid feed.
Varieties For digestibility: Burpless hybrids. For length: Kyoto, Chinese Long Green. For limited space: Patio-Pik. For earliness: Kaga.

Chicory

Indoor cucumber

Outdoor cucumber

LETTUCES

For summer crops sow in spring, under cloches and then in the open, following with successive small sowings until mid-summer. For autumn crops sow after mid-summer and protect with cloches as necessary. For late autumn and early winter sow in the greenhouse border in late summer. For spring use sow under cloches or in the cold greenhouse in autumn, or grow winter-hardies in the open

Lettuces require plenty of organic matter in the soil and summer crops benefit from pre-sowing dressings of fertilizer and from liquid feeds. Poor soil, lack of moisture and overcrowding are the chief causes of bolting and failure to heart. Thin early and for preference use pelleted seed. Thinning of autumn-sown crops under cloches or in the open may be left until spring to allow for winter losses. Plants bought from the nurseryman succeed early in the season but are difficult to establish later on and usually bolt.

Varieties There are four distinct types: round or flat cabbage, curly cabbage, leafy or non-hearting, and cos. Spring sowing: Unrivalled, All the Year Round, Little Gem (cos), Tom Thumb. Summer sowing: Continuity, Avondefiance, Webbs Wonderful, Buttercrunch. (The last two are crisp or curly types.) Autumn sowing: In the open, Winter Density, Valdor. Under cloches, May King, Premier. In the greenhouse, Kwiek for winter, Kloek for spring. Non-heartening, Salad Bowl.

RADISHES

The fastest growing salad crop after mustard and cress and a useful filler up of unused corners. In theory very simple to grow, in practice usually grown very badly.

Sow little and often and allow each root plenty of room. Sowing may start in very early spring under cloches and continue at three-weekly intervals until well into the autumn. Sow very thinly in a wide drill and thin the seedlings to 2cm apart as soon as they can be handled. Pull roots as they reach usable size, even though still small. The aim is a wide row with every root having room to expand.

Any soil manured for previous crops will grow good radishes. Moisture is vitally important, as radishes are not deeprooting and dry soil results in hot, tough roots. In dry weather water the drill before sowing and keep crop moist.

Varieties Saxerre, Red Forcing, Sparkler, Cherry Belle, French Breakfast. The first two for early sowing and quick growth, the last for quality.

SALAD ONIONS

A limited supply of spring or salad onions is provided by thinnings from the bulb onion crop. Special sowings of salad onions are, however, worthwhile for those who are fond of them. The true salad onion retains a straight, tender stem for much longer than the bulbing varieties. Too much reliance on thinnings also often means that bulb crop is left overcrowded to maintain the supply.

Salad onions are easy to grow at any time from spring to autumn. A fine tilth and a little fertilizer raked in before sowing are the only soil preparation needed. Sow fairly thinly and cover the seed lightly. Water freely in dry weather.

The earliest pullings are from autumn-sown crops, which succeed in the open in favoured districts and on the lighter soils. Elsewhere they need cloche protection. Sow very sparingly in widely spaced rows so that air circulates between the plants and keeps them dry enough to prevent a destructive outbreak of mildew.

Varieties White Lisbon, White Spanish.

TOMATOES, INDOOR

An important greenhouse crop. Under glass it is a virtual certainty, but in the open it is dependent on the weather.

Lettuces

Radish

Salad onion

Tomato seed, even with some warmth, should not be sown until early spring. Don't plant while night frosts persist even though temperatures are high in daytime sunlight. Conserve heat as much as possible in the first weeks after planting, opening ventilators only when the interior temperature exceeds 21°C and closing them some hours before sunset.

Growing in the border: Dig deeply in winter, working in a little compost or peat and a very light dressing compound fertilizer before planting. After a few years the risk of disease increases and the soil must be replaced or sterilized or the crop grown in containers.

Growing in containers Grow in 25cm pots filled to within 8cm of the rim with potting compost, adding more compost when roots appear on the surface. Water very frequently in hot weather. For ring culture, grow in bottomless tompots standing on a bed of peat, clinker or coarse sand and filled with potting compost. The standing bed is soaked at intervals and liquid feed given in the tompots. To grow in bags, allow two to four plants per bag according to size. The bags must not be allowed to dry out and are unsuitable for the greenhouse left unattended for the day unless some form of automatic watering is installed.

Feed plants, however grown, twice weekly with a high-potash liquid fertilizer. Support on strings or canes, remove sideshoots and pinch out growing points when the roof is reached.

Ventilate freely in hot weather and spray overhead occasionally to aid pollination.

Varieties Moneymaker, Ware Cross, Supercross, Ailsa Craig. For the heated house: Eurocross. Large Continental types of exceptional quality: Big Boy, Marmand.

TOMATOES, OUTDOOR

Tall varieties of tomato are grown as a single stem, side shoots being removed and the plants stopped when three or four trusses have set. Dwarf or bush varieties have a spreading habit and carry a number of trusses on branches close to the ground. They may be covered with large cloches even when fully grown.

Choose the sunniest and most sheltered site available. Soil should be well dug and well drained but not freshly manured. The plants should be fed weekly with a high-potash liquid fertilizer only after the first truss has set. Too much vigorous leafy growth is not wanted.

Buy or raise plants in the greenhouse, not sowing until a night minimum temperature of at least 10°C is assured. Prick out as soon as the seedlings can be handled, grow on close to the glass and harden-off thoroughly. Plant out when there is no risk of frost and during a warm, quiet spell.

Stake and tie tall varieties when planted. Rub out all side-shoots while small. Stop the plant when three trusses have set or six weeks before the first frost is expected.

Bush varieties tend to become overcrowded with branches and fruit. Restrict the main branches to three and rub out superfluous side-shoots. If the plants are to be cloched they must be kept to a reasonable size. Support ripening trusses clear of the ground on forked twigs or grow on a strip of black polythene.

Varieties Tall: Moneymaker, Outdoor Girl, Ailsa Craig. Bush: Sleaford Abundance, Sigmabush, Primabel, The Amateur. Small fruited, for cloches or pots on the patio: Tiny Tim, Gardener's Delight.

▼ A truss of ripe tomatoes.

MISCELLANEOUS CROPS: ARTICHOKES, GLOBE

A half-hardy, short-lived perennial, grown for its large edible flower buds.

Prepare the soil by digging deeply in winter, breaking up the subsoil to improve drainage and working in some organic manure. Leave the soil rough to weather to a tilth and before planting fork in a small handful of a compound fertilizer for each plant.

Buy plants in spring; it takes too long to raise them from seed. Plant, water and weed carefully; the small plants are easily mistaken for thistles. Feed fortnightly with liquid fertilizer from mid-summer onwards. Only small heads are produced the first year.

Cover the crowns with protective material when the tops die down in autumn. Peat, covered by a cloche to keep it dry, is effective even against severe frost.

Plants last about four years. In the third year, take basal suckers in spring, pot them up in soil-less compost and plant out when fully rooted. Suckers may also be taken in autumn and overwintered in the greenhouse.

Gather the heads before the scales turn purple. Secondary buds develop after the main ones are cut.

Varieties Usually a case of Hobson's Choice. Get Gros Vert de Laon if possible.

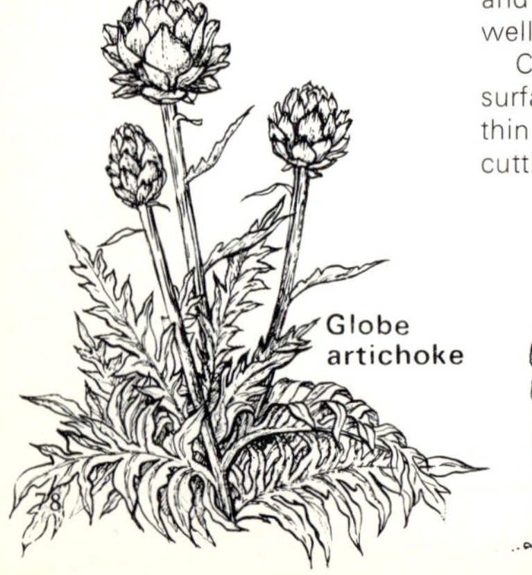
Globe artichoke

ASPARAGUS

The only important perennial vegetable crop. Rated a luxury, but hardy and a good investment. An asparagus bed can remain in bearing for 20 years.

Formerly grown on raised beds, asparagus is now frequently planted in single rows on the flat. Prepare the site in winter. Put down a line and dig a 60cm wide strip along it, breaking up the subsoil and working in a barrowload of manure or compost to every 1m of row. Work to a good tilth in spring, incorporating 60g of compound fertilizer per 1m of row.

Order two-year-old roots for spring delivery. They are sent when starting into growth and must be planted at once. They must never be left exposed to sun and wind. Take out a trench some 20cm deep and form a ridge of soil along the bottom. Set the asparagus crowns astride the ridge with roots pointing downwards and fill in. The tops of the crowns should be 8cm below the surface.

Cut no shoots the first year. Give water and liquid feeds to build up the plants. Hand weed thoroughly. Remove the 'fern' when it turns yellow in autumn and top dress the tow with well rotted manure or compost.

Cut shoots just below the surface, cut them all including thin mis-shapen ones, and stop cutting by mid-summer.

Varieties Not important, but try to get all-male plants which are more productive.

Asparagus

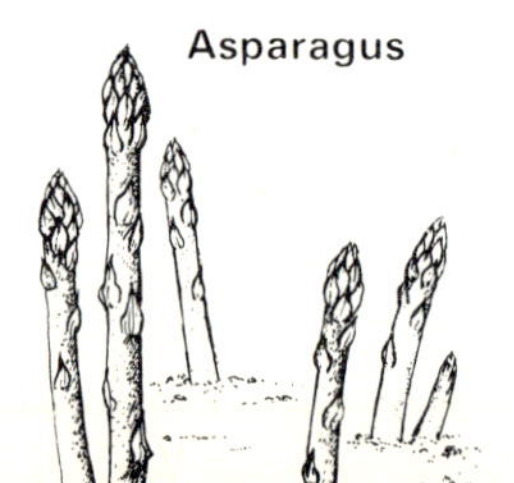

AUBERGINES

The aubergine or egg plant is interesting but uneconomic. In temperate climates and average summers it rarely succeeds in the open. It fruits in the cold greenhouse but yields only four fruits per plant.

A night minimum of 16°C is required for germination and the day temperature should also remain above that level for the seedlings to grow. Without some form of heat a start cannot be made in the greenhouse until late spring or early summer. A heated propagator saves time as germination is slow.

Prick out the seedlings singly into small pots and grow on until they have about four leaves. Transplant into 20cm pots of soil-less potting compost.

Maintain an equable temperature by closing ventilators on cool nights. Keep well watered and never allow the compost to dry out. Stop the plants when they reach a height of 20cm. Allow two laterals to develop and stop them when each has two fruits set and swelling. Remove all other fruits and shoots. Feed weekly with liquid fertilizer.

Varieties Long Purple, Early Long Purple, New York. The last two may be attempted outdoors in a warm, sunny position provided they have cloche protection.

Aubergines

CELERIAC

Irregular turnip-shaped roots with a strong celery flavour. Used as a celery substitute in cooking but unsuitable for salads. May be lifted and stored for winter.

Without a moist, fertile soil the roots are small and stringy and on dry chalks celeriac is not worth growing. Dig in any available manure or peat supplemented by a dressing of a compound fertilizer before planting.

You may not be able to buy plants. Sow in the greenhouse in spring when a minimum of 10°C can be maintained. Prick out early into trays of potting compost and plant out after hardening off.

Plant out in a wide, shallow drill with the bulblet at the base of the seedling resting on the surface. Planting in a drill makes it easier to give the growing plants a thorough soaking, which may be necessary at intervals in a dry season. If growth appears to be slow give a fortnightly liquid feed. Remove all suckers and shoots appearing on the bulb itself. Lift and store when the tops die down in autumn.

Varieties The old varieties are of indifferent quality and appearance. Choose the new introduction, Globus.

HERBS

Culinary herbs are of increasing importance.

Chives Herbaceous perennial, clump of many small bulbs. Dies down in winter, may be potted up and forwarded indoors. Soil, well drained. Position, sunny. Propagation, seed or division of clumps.

Mint Perennial. Two main species, spearmint and apple mint, latter very vigorous. Spearmint may be grown in pots. Soil, moist. Position, sun or partial shade. Propagate by division of rhizomes.

Parsley Biennial, treated as an annual. Best cloched in winter. Pot up while small for house or greenhouse. Soil, good as possible. Position, sun or partial shade. Propagate by seed sown in spring or summer.

Sage Hardy shrub, medium size, decorative flowers. Suitable for drying. Soil, well drained. Position, full sun, sheltered from cold winds. Propagate by seed or cuttings in summer.

Thyme Hardy prostrate shrub, ornamental in flower. Many species. Suitable for drying. Soil, well drained. Position, full sun. Propagate by seed or cuttings in summer.

MARROWS AND COURGETTES

All varieties are sensitive to frost and must not be sown or planted in the open while it is a possibility. Courgettes are

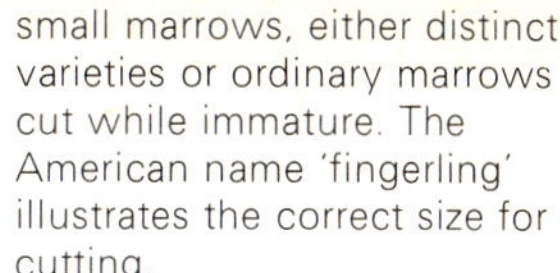

small marrows, either distinct varieties or ordinary marrows cut while immature. The American name 'fingerling' illustrates the correct size for cutting.

Prepare a site for each plant in a sheltered and sunny position. Dig a hole one spit deep, mix the soil with an equal quantity of garden compost or rotted manure and refill the hole with it. Marrows can be grown on a matured compost heap if provided with a 15cm depth of soil. The compost does not suffer but is of course not available until the marrows have finished.

Sow under glass a month before planting-out time, three seeds to a 7-cm peat pot, reducing to one seedling. Or sow three seeds direct on each site, again reducing to one plant. Avoid root disturbance when planting. Protect young plants with slug pellets.

Keep well watered and hand pollinate if fruits fail to swell. Gather marrows while small to encourage continued cropping, only fruits for winter storage being left to grow large and ripen.

Bush types are compact and may be cloched for a time to promote earlier cropping. Trailers may be trained up fences or other supports.

Varieties Bush: Zucchini (early), Green Bush, Smallpak. Trailers: Long Green, Long White, Table Dainty. Courgettes: Green Bush Hybrid.

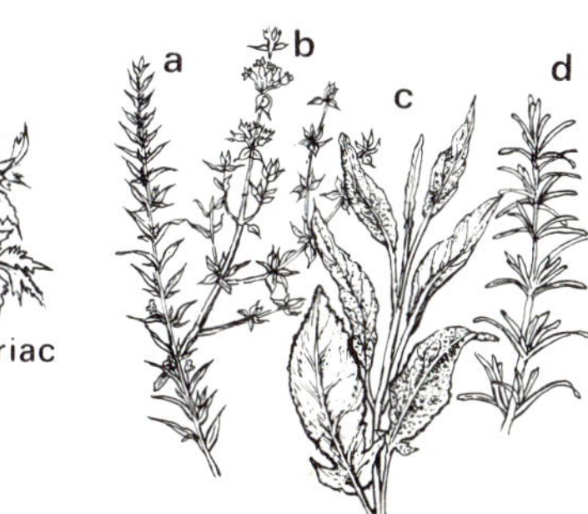

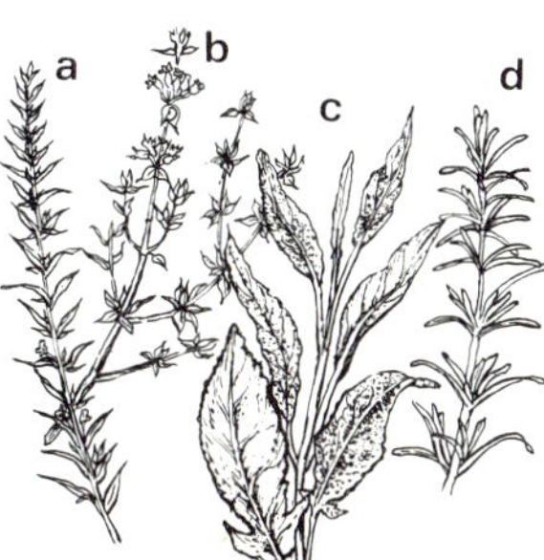

▼ Herbs
a winter savoury
b thyme
c sage
d rosemary

MUSHROOMS

Mushrooms are grown in beds of composted straw, indoors and at any time of year. They do not need light. They do not reproduce by seed but by minute spores, supplied as a culture known as 'spawn'.

The mushroom bed
Traditionally it is composed of strawy stable manure, stacked and turned until composted to a moist, friable material. Baled straw and a chemical activator may be used instead. The bales are soaked with water, then opened and stacked as described for garden compost, each 10cm layer being sprinkled with activator.

The bed is made up 25cm deep on the floor of an outhouse or cellar. Ideal temperature is 10-15°C but a wide variation is tolerated. The bed must be out of direct sunlight but total darkness is unnecessary. Make the bed firm and cover with newspapers to conserve moisture.

Spawning Every packet of spawn carries detailed instructions. Briefly, the bed is spawned when its temperature remains below 21°C. Holes are made 20cm apart in the compost, a small piece of spawn placed in each and the compost pressed round it.

A week or two later the white threads of mycelium, the vegetative part of the mushroom, spread through the compost. The bed is then covered with a 5cm 'casing' of sifted subsoil or peat mixed with a little ground limestone. The casing is kept moist but water is not allowed to reach the compost.

After a few more weeks clusters of tiny 'pinheads' form in the casing and full-sized mushrooms develop from them. Production is not continuous but comes in flushes over a long period.

Varieties All spawns are pure cultures of the cultivated mushroom.

SEAKALE BEET

A tasty vegetable resembling perpetual spinach, and the green part of the leaf may be used in the same way. The main edible part, however, is the broad leaf stalk and midrib, pure white or rhubarb pink according to variety.

The crop is not fully hardy, it is best sown in late spring and used before the advent of autumn frosts. The plant is attractive in appearance and a group in the flower border is inoffensive and yields many pickings. The outer leaves are cut at ground level and more are produced from the centre, though the stems get progressively smaller.

Good soil is needed for rapid and succulent growth. Dig in any kind of manure and before sowing rake in 30g per sq m of sulphate of ammonia. Sow thinly and keep thinned. For really fine stems the plants should at all times be only just touching. A fortnightly liquid feed from the time cutting begins helps to maintain growth.

Varieties The white form is listed as Seakale Beet, or Silver Beet and must not be confused with Spinach Beet. The pink form is listed as Ruby Chard.

SPINACH

Collective name for several botanically different plants providing edible leaves.

Round or summer spinach
Annual, fairly hardy. Sow in spring and monthly for succession. Soil; well dug and if possible manured, with a pre-sowing dressing of fertilizer. Sow very thinly in a wide drill, using thinnings when large enough. Water freely. Succeeds in partial shade.

Prickly spinach Annual, hardy, sown in early autumn it lasts until severe frosts. Name refers to seed. Requires well drained soil and sheltered position

Perpetual spinach Hardy biennial. Sow on any good soil in summer in narrow drills, thinning early and giving plants plenty of room. Protect from birds. Used from autumn to spring, especially if cloched. Cut down flower stems in spring to prolong cropping.

New Zealand spinach
Tender, suitable for light, dry soils where ordinary summer spinach runs to seed. Sow under glass in spring and plant out when safe from frost. Growth is semi-prostrate and plants must be well spaced. Pick leaves as required.

Varieties Summer: Monarch, Long-standing Round. Prickly-seeded: Greenmarket, Long-standing Prickly. Perpetual Spinach is also listed as Spinach Beet.

Seakale beet

Spinach

Mushrooms

SWEETCORN

A quick growing type of maize, the cobs being used as vegetables before the sugar in the kernels is converted into starch by ripening.

The crop does not stand frost and, being tall and surface-rooting, suffers in high winds. Choose a sheltered site in full sun and in cold districts grow a suitable variety.

Good soil is needed for rapid growth and well filled cobs. Dig in organic manure followed by a 80g per sq m dressing of compound fertilizer before planting.

Although seeds may be sown direct it pays to start the plants in greenhouse or frame, using peat pots and the same methods as for marrows and other tender crops. Plant in a block of short rows to ensure fertilization by the wind-borne pollen. Protect from birds. Water in dry weather and mulch with peat or garden compost. Harvest when the contents of the kernels is the consistency of thin cream.

Varieties For heavy crop: John Innes Hybrid, Kelvedon Glory, Golden Bantam. For cold districts: North Star, Polar Vee. For earliness: First of All, Earliking, Extra Early Sweet.

SQUASHES

The squash is a relative of the marrow, apparently originating in the United States. Nutritionally, it is probably the more valuable of the two, but it may be slightly less hardy than the marrow. It prefers hot summers to cool, damp ones and appreciates the protection of cloches when first planted out.

Prepare the soil of planting sites as advised for marrows, forming a small mound for each plant. Trailing squashes are less rampant than trailing marrows, the fruits are on the whole smaller and some are oddly shaped. They can therefore be treated as slightly decorative climbers if ground space is limited. But they must not be confused with ornamental gourds, which are highly decorative but quite uneatable.

Raise plants under glass in the same way as marrows. If you sow direct on the planting site wait for a spell of warm weather. Cover the seeds with jam jars until germination if no cloches are available. This is also worth doing with outdoor sowings of cucumbers and marrows.

Give plenty of water and a fortnightly liquid feed when fruiting. Harvest summer varieties regularly but leave winter squashes on the vine to ripen for storing.

Varieties Summer: Vegetable Spaghetti, Baby Crookneck, Sweet Dumpling. Winter: Butternut, Hubbard Squash, Gold Nugget.

BLACKBERRIES

The blackberry is among the hardiest of soft fruits, happy on all soils but the very driest, late-flowering and unaffected by spring frosts. It does, however, need a lot of space and is not a first choice for the small garden.

Prepare the ground by digging in some rotted manure or compost to assist maximum growth in the first year, on most soils little subsequent manuring is necessary. Plant in autumn if possible, cutting back the canes. In spring, fork in a handful of a compound fertilizer round each plant and keep well watered and clear of large weeds.

Take great care of young canes training them immediately on permanent supports. They are very brittle and once broken are not replaced until the following year.

Varieties Himalayan Giant, Bedford Giant, Parsley-leaved, Merton Thornless (most manageable), John Innes (very late).

▼ Blackberries ready for picking.

BLACKCURRANTS

The site should have some shelter from cold winds and not be notorious for spring frosts. Place sacking or other material over the bushes on a cold night.

Dig and manure the soil before planting. Plant two-year-old bushes, preferably in autumn and cut them back. In spring fork in a little fertilizer and mulch with manure or compost. New growth from the base is essential for sustained cropping and the bushes respond to nitrogenous manures. Apply an annual spring dressing of 30g of sulphate of ammonia per bush, followed by a mulch.

Hand weed or hoe with care. Cut out some of the old, dark-coloured branches every year.

Propagation is by 20cm long cuttings of young, ripe wood, with all the buds left on, inserted in sandy soil in autumn. Leave three buds showing.

Varieties Early and mid-season: Wellington XXX, Boskoop Giant, Top Cross. Late: Daniels September, Amos Black, Westwick Choice.

GOOSEBERRIES

The gooseberry tolerates partial shade. It flowers early and is susceptible to spring frosts. Keep some dry covering material handy during the crucial period. It is a good choice for the heavier soils, and if the ground is well drained and well dug and manured initially seems to manage with little attention beyond weeding and pruning. On light soils the crop may suffer from potash deficiency, with poor growth and productivity. Apply 30g of sulphate of potash or 80g of a compound fertilizer per bush, lightly forking it in.

Propagate by 30cm long cuttings of young wood, taken in the autumn and inserted in sandy soil to a depth of about 10cm. All but the top four buds are removed, leaving a length of bare stem to form the 'leg'. The buds develop into the main branches.

Varieties Culinary: Keepsake, Whinham's Industry, Careless. Dessert: Leveller, Lancer. The last is also a fine late cooking variety.

HYBRID BERRIES

A number of cane fruits have, like the loganberry, resulted from a raspberry/blackberry cross. The following are well worth growing, treated exactly the same as the logan or blackberry.

The boysenberry has canes about 2m long and is a most consistant cropper. The fruit is long, very dark red, slightly acid and makes superb jam.

The veitchberry is also a moderate grower. It fruits after raspberries and the berry resembles a mulberry-coloured blackberry but is twice as large.

The Worcester berry is a bush fruit and is probably an American wild gooseberry. The berries, reddish purple, have a pleasant flavour suggestive of blackcurrant.

The Japanese wineberry is a cane fruit but not a hybrid. The canes not more than 2m long are covered with short red hairs and are very decorative. The berries, small and amber yellow, are sweet and refreshing.

LOGANBERRIES

The loganberry is a blackberry/raspberry hybrid and is cultivated in exactly the same way as the blackberry.

Loganberries and black-berries are easily propagated by tip-layering. A cane of the current year's growth is bent down and the tip buried in a shallow hole. This is done in late summer, and by the following spring the tip will have rooted and begun to make new growth. It is cut from the parent plant in autumn and planted out.

Varieties The most reliable is the virus-free LY59.

RASPBERRIES

The raspberry does well in districts with relatively cool, damp summers. It tolerates a certain amount of shade,

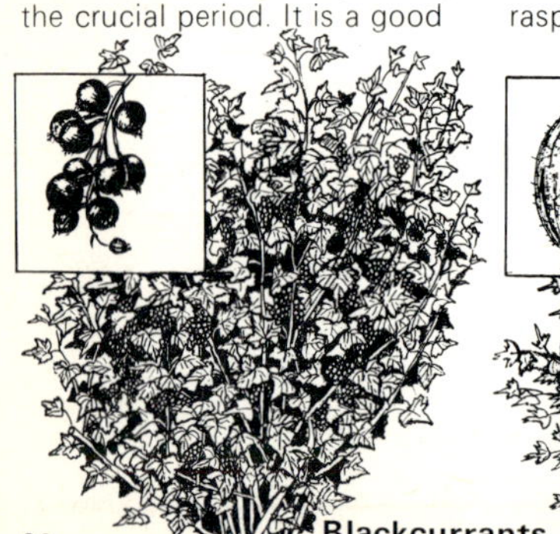
Blackcurrants

Gooseberries

Loganberri

flowers late enough to escape spring frosts and is quite long-lived.

The ideal soil is moist and full of humus. The raspberry's roots are extensive but near the surface, it suffers from drought and from deep digging near the canes. Control weeds by hoeing. Mulch every spring with manure, compost or peat. A good layer of organic matter, added to annually, is a prime factor in raspberry growing.

Cut out the old canes immediately after fruiting. Reduce the number of new canes to six per clump.

Propagation is by suckers, the canes that spring up some distance from the main clump. They are allowed to grow during the summer, and lifted and severed from the parent clump when fully rooted in autumn.

Varieties Early: Malling Promise, Malling Jewel. Late: Lloyd George, Norfolk Giant. Autumn-fruiting: September, Zeva.

RED AND WHITE CURRANTS

Treat these in the same manner. The white currant fruits on young wood, the red currant on fruiting spurs on mature branches.

The site should have shelter from strong winds; redcurrant wood is extremely brittle. Most soils are suitable, but bushes on light land should receive an annual spring dressing of 30g of sulphate of potash each, followed by a mulch of manure or compost.

The two-year-old bushes normally planted will not have many branches. Allow more to develop, including any starting near the top of the leg, though otherwise it is kept clear of growth. All suckers from ground level are removed.

Propagation is by cuttings treated like those of the gooseberry. Fairly easy.

Varieties Red: Laxton's No. 1, Jonkheer van Tets. White: White Versailles.

STRAWBERRIES

Summer fruiting varieties tolerate some shade, autumn fruiters need full sun to ripen. Soil must contain plenty of organic matter in any form.

Three distinct types are grown. Summer fruiters, providing the main crop, are planted in late summer or very early autumn to fruit the following summer. Perpetuals are planted in autumn or spring to fruit the following summer and autumn, but are disbudded until mid-summer. Alpines are planted in spring or summer and fruit within a few weeks.

For maximum yield, grow summer fruiters as a matted row. Plant two rows 60cm apart, with 30cm between plants. Allow runners to root and form a strip of mixed old and young plants by the second year. For cloching start with the plants 22cm apart.

Plant perpetuals 45cm apart in the rows with the rows 1m apart. They form massive clumps and even fruit on unrooted runners.

Plant alpines 20cm apart in groups or as edgings. They are easily raised from seed. Both the other types are propagated from runners. Protect from birds with temporary netting or grow in a fruit cage. Alpines are the exception and suffer little bird damage. Summer fruiters are cloched in early spring, perpetuals in autumn to prolong ripening. Hand weed matted rows, water in dry weather while berries are swelling. Keep berries from contact with the soil by the use of straw, polythene, dry peat under cloches, or wire supports.

Varieties Summer fruiters: Early, Cambridge Vigour. All-round performance: Cambridge Favourite. Quality: Royal Sovereign. Size of berry: Grandee. Late: Cambridge Late Pine. Perpetuals: Sans Rivale, Hampshire Maid, Gento. Alpines: Baron Solemacher, Alexandra.

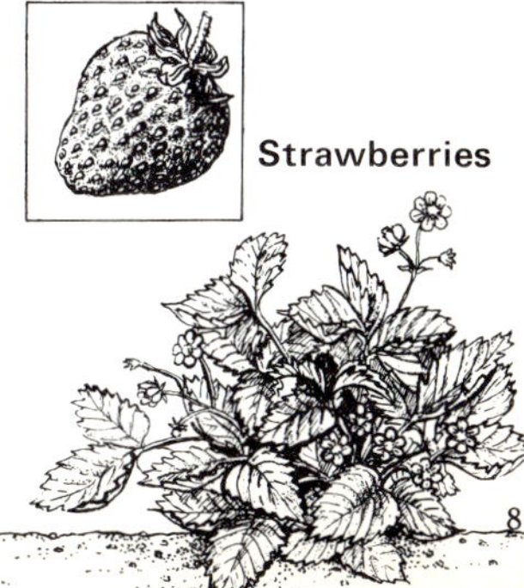

TOP FRUIT: APPLES

Apples are very hardy and are grown over the whole range of temperate climates. Dry, sunny summers produce the highest quality dessert fruit, cookers are much less choosey.

Soil should be well drained and not too fertile; nitrogenous manures, organic or chemical, are rarely needed. Apples often fruit better planted on a grass plot or on the lawn than in cultivated soil, the grass mopping up excess nitrogen.

Give trees a good start by careful planting and staking. Nurse them through the first growing season with watering and overhead spraying when necessary.

Varieties Consult a good nursery some months before planting time. The following is a small selection based on general reliability and quality: Early dessert, Discovery, Lady Sudeley, Tydemans Worcester, Laxtons Fortune, James Grieve. The last is also a good cooker and is frost-resistant. Dessert keepers, autumn and winter: Ellisons Orange, Winston, Crispin, Spartan, Merton Russet, Golden Delicious. Early cookers: Arthur Turner, Grenadier, Early Victoria. Keeping cookers, autumn and winter: Lord Derby, Annie Elizabeth, Edward VII, Bramley Seedling, Newton Wonder, Crawley Beauty.

CHERRIES

Sweet cherries are not for the average garden since no dwarfing stock is yet available and a standard or half-standard tree takes 10-15 years to come into bearing.

The acid cherry, Morello, is self-fertile and may be grown as a single fan-trained tree on a north-facing wall. It is about the only fruit to succeed in that position and a most valuable one.

Soil must contain plenty of lime and the planting site be well prepared. Dig in old manure or compost and a double handful of bone meal. After autumn planting apply a thick peat mulch to reduce the penetration of frost. Maintain the mulch permanently and keep the soil uniformly moist. Cherries react badly to alternations of wet and dry.

Prune in the same way as peaches and nectarines (See 'The cultivation of fruit'). The crop is borne on shoots of the previous season's growth and in the mature tree these are restricted to replacement shoots to prevent over-crowding.

Varieties Morello, a red form called Kentish Red, and a semi-sweet but apparently self-fertile variety called May Duke.

GRAPES

The grape vine is extremely hardy, the obstacle to its cultivation in cooler climates being the need for fine, warm weather in autumn. It prefers a sharply contrasting climate with hard winters and hot summers.

The site should be in full sun, preferably backed by a wall or fence. Soil should be well drained and poor rather than fertile.

Vines must be pruned if they are not to run wild and be unfruitful. Do this by cutting back the autumn-planted vine to four buds or 'eyes' in spring. Keep the two strongest growths and tie them to wall nails or a trellis. In the autumn cut one back to two eyes, the other to about seven eyes. Allow fruiting laterals to develop on the latter and after it has fruited cut it out. Train up two replacement canes from the two eyes left on the other growth, and in the autumn repeat the process. Thus you always have a short young cane with fruiting laterals and another ready to replace it in autumn.

Varieties Many new introductions are on trial and you should consult a specialist supplier. Suggested dessert varieties are: Buckland Sweetwater, Royal Burgundy Muscadine and Miller's Burgundy. For wine, Muller.

PEACHES AND NECTARINES

Almost the only difference between them is in the downy skin of the peach.

The peach is hardy but has the disadvantage of flowering and is vulnerable to spring frosts. Trees of bush form may be grown in open ground in favoured districts but the fan-trained tree on a sunny wall generally gives the best results.

The best soil is an average medium loam. However, when planting on heavy clay remove a spit's depth of subsoil from the planting hole and replace it with coarse ballast covered with chopped turf and topsoil before planting. Mulch wall trees and water when necessary. Soil at the foot of a wall is usually drier than elsewhere and an irregular water supply is a frequent cause of fruit dropping.

Prune wall trees regularly and tie in new growth. Thin very heavy crops, first to about 10cm when the fruit is as big as a hazel nut, then to twice that distance when the size of a walnut. Leave the crop spaced as evenly as possible over the tree.

Varieties In order of ripening. Peaches: Hale's Early, Peregrin, Duke of York. Nectarines: Early Rivers, Lord Napier, Pineapple.

PEARS

The finest pears are from warm and sheltered conditions, and for these reasons wall trees often give better results than free-standing forms. Several single-stem cordons, planted against a south or west wall, take up very little room. If of different varieties there are no pollination problems and a long season of use is possible.

A good medium garden soil is suitable. On heavy clays break up the subsoil, and on very light land dig in plenty of mature garden compost or well-decayed manure when preparing the site. Add a double handful of bone meal when planting.

Prune systematically, summer-pruning cordons by nipping back the laterals to induce a mass of stubby fruiting spurs. Protect blossom from frost by covering with old curtains or other material where practicable.

Varieties For a single self-fertile dessert variety: Conference. Early to mid-season dessert: Williams Bon Chretien, Packhams Triumph, Improved Fertility. Long-keeping dessert: Winter Nelis, Josephine de Malines. Culinary: Pitmaston Duchess (dual purpose, very large), Catillac. The finest dessert pear, Doyenne du Comice, is unreliable. Catillac is a fine cooker.

PLUMS, GAGES AND DAMSONS

The plum family is hardy and tolerant. The gages are the least reliable, sometimes missing a crop several years in succession.

Plums do better on chalk soils. On the poorest they benefit from an annual dressing of compound fertilizer and on all soils from mulching and thorough soakings in dry weather.

Boughs visibly drooping under the weight of fruit should be supported. If a break occurs, trim the branch to a level surface and paint it immediately. Simple precautions like this, with pruning restricted to the summer months, are the best safeguard against silver leaf disease. Aphid infestation is easily controlled by a tar oil winter wash.

Varieties For a single tree of a self-fertile culinary and dessert variety the choice is Victoria. Others either require, or give better results with, a pollinator. Early cookers: Rivers Early Prolific, Czar, Early Laxton. Early dessert: Severn Cross. Later culinary: Belle de Louvain, Monarch, Purple Pershore, Marjorie's Seedling. Gages: Early Transparent, Cambridge Gage. Outstanding quality dessert plums: Coe's Golden Drop, Jefferson's Gage. Damsons: Merryweather, Shropshire Prune, Bradley's King.

Conversion tables

Length

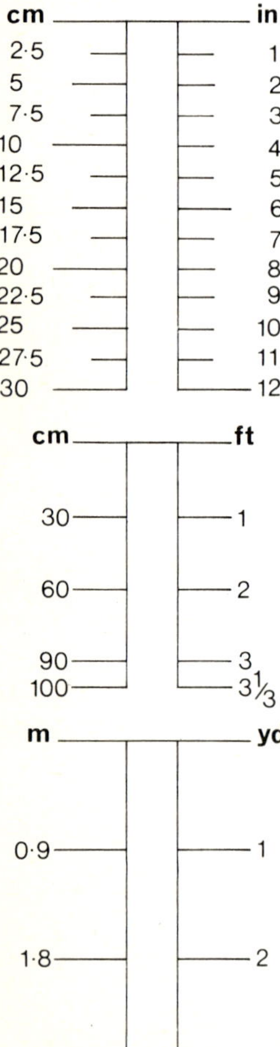

Area

1sq cm = 0.15sq in
6.45sq cm = 1sq in
1sq m = 10.76sq ft/ 1.19sq yd
4046sq m = 1 acre
1 hectare = 2.47 acres

Weight

1g = 0.035oz
28.35g = 1oz
100g = 3.5oz
454g = 1lb
500g = 17.5oz
1kg = 2.21lb
6.35kg = 1 stone/14lb
50.80kg = 1cwt/112lb
1.02 tonnes = 1 ton

Capacity and Volume

500ml = 0.88pt
568ml = 1pt
1000ml = 1.76pt
1 litre = 35.19fl oz
4.55 litres = 1gal
10 litres (1dl) = 2.2gal
1 bushel/8gal = 36.37 litres
100 litres = 22gal
1cu cm = 0.06cu in
1cu dm = 0.035cu ft
1cu m = 1.31cu yd

Abbreviations

sq = square
g = gram
oz = ounce
kg = kilogram
lb = pound
cwt = hundredweight
ml = millilitre (=cc)
pt = pint
l = litre
fl oz = fluid ounce
dl = decolitre
gal = gallon
hl = hectolitre
cu = cubic
dm = decimetre
cm = centimetre
mm = millimetre
m = metre
in = inch
ft = foot
yd = yard

Temperature

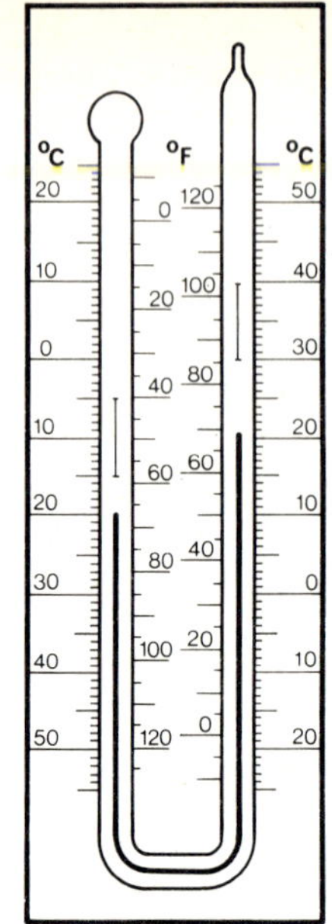

▲ A maximum and minimum thermometer is used to record the highest and lowest temperatures every 24 hours.

°F = °Fahrenheit
°C = °Celcius (Centigrade)
* = freezing point

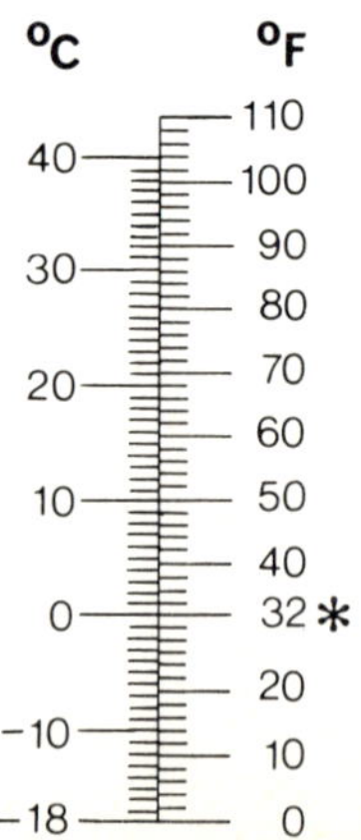

Societies

The joy of gardening is that there are no limits at either end of the scale of learning. Right from the start a newcomer to the horticultural world can derive much pleasure from sowing the first packet of seeds, even if the sowing only results in a box of cress. Such an experience opens your account of horticultural knowledge and from then on, if you so desire, your background of experience can be built up by acquiring theoretical knowledge and practical experience.

So far this book has attempted to outline the possibilities for both vegetable and fruit growing in the home garden and on the allotment. If you have been encouraged to take a deeper interest in the subject you will be joining no less than 14 million UK gardeners, some of whom will wish to share their hobby and experience with you.

In practically every district in the country, no matter how remote, there is within easy reach a horticultural society, groups of people with a common interest in gardening.

Most societies are founded on a broad basis and their activities cover not only fruit and vegetables but flowers, shrubs and trees as well.

In addition to shows at which the members demonstrate their skills by entering home-grown produce or flowers in competitive classes, the societies arrange meetings, during the autumn and winter period, at which horticultural specialists speak and illustrate with slides their own particular facets of horticultural knowledge.

Some societies have trading sections which buy seeds, fertilizers, etc. in bulk. Their members are then able to purchase the smaller quantities they need at discount prices. These concessions considerably reduce the cost of gardening for the privileged members.

In addition, many societies arrange visits to gardens of great interest. Such outings, shows and lectures would quickly bring you in close contact with the keenest of the local gardeners, who throughout the country have a reputation for wishing to share their experience and expertise with the up-and-coming gardener.

ALLOTMENT SOCIETIES

With the greatly increased interest in vegetable growing, Allotment Societies are thriving, and they too are widely spread throughout the country. The largest and most active Allotment Societies are often found in urban areas where undeveloped land is more scarce and gardens behind the houses are often much smaller than their counterparts in the villages. Allotment Societies are usually involved with a single site or group of allotments, although larger societies covering several sites are in existence. They work on a similar basis to the Horticultural Societies but in addition they campaign for more sites in certain areas. If you have difficulty in locating a nearby Allotment Society you can contact your local authority office or write to:

The Secretary,
The National Allotments and Leisure Gardens Society Ltd,
22 High Street,
Flitwick,
Bedford MK45 1DT
Telephone: 05257-2361
asking for particulars of your nearest branch.

With waiting lists for allotments in most towns and cities it is necessary to get on the waiting list as soon as possible. While some Allotment Societies are responsible for the lettings, in many cases the application should be made through the local authority.

The National Vegetable Society

The National Vegetable Society through its annual handbook and leaflets affords keen vegetable growers a wealth of information for a nominal annual membership fee of £1.50. The secretary is
Mr A. Scot,
8 Hazelwood Mansions,
Rostrevor Road,
London SW6
Telephone: 01-736 0332.

Separate branches of the society operate actively in the following areas and can be contacted through their secretaries at the following addresses:

Southern Branch
Mr W. E. Kingshot
5 Fowlers Croft,
Compton,
Guildford GU3 1EH.

Midland Branch
Mrs M. D. King,
Gretton Cottage,
Campden House Estate,
Chipping Campden,
Glos. GL55 8UP.

Northern Branch
Mr W. R. Hargreaves,
29 Revidge Road,
Blackburn,
Lancs.
Telephone: 0254-64989.

Scottish Branch:
Mr R. E. Wood,
33 Orchard Road,
Edinburgh EH4 2EP.
Telephone: 031-332 6319.

A note to your area branch secretary would immediately bring you in contact with other gardeners and all the up-to-date information on local vegetable growing. In the North of England where the National Vegetable Society is particularly strong, District Associations operate. Information about their activities can be obtained from the following addresses:

South Yorkshire:
Mr M. H. Evans,
56 Jenkin Road,
Horbury, nr. Wakefield.

West Yorkshire:
Mr H. McCartney,
21 Upper Rushton Road,
Thornbury,
Bradford BD3 7HH.

East Yorkshire:
Mr B. Taylor,
861 Spring Bank West,
Hull.

Manchester District:
Mr W. T. A. Burrows,
64 Pelham Road,
Thelwall, nr. Warrington.

Lincoln District:
Mr R. Good,
69 Sunfield Crescent,
Birchwood Estate,
Lincoln.

East Lancashire:
Mr G. McManus,
1 Pickering Fold,
Roman Road,
Blackburn.

Merseyside:
Mr R. H. Dodd,
71 Frankby Road,
Newton,
West Kirby,
Wirral L48 6EQ.

North East Derbyshire:
Mr R. Hill,
2 Snape Hill,
Dronfield,
Sheffield.

Many local Horticultural Societies are affiliated to the National Vegetable Society and members of such societies are able in a limited way to benefit from such an arrangement.

The Royal Horticultural Society

The Royal Horticultural Society or the RHS is the major society in Great Britain. Its activities are broadly based, covering every facet of horticultural practice from growing the humble potato to the extravagance of cultivating orchids. The Chelsea Flower Show, held in London each May, has an international reputation. Although vegetables and fruit are not featured extensively the exhibits staged by the National Farmers Union are an education in vegetable and fruit growing, as are the technical and the scientific stands manned by personnel from the RHS laboratories at Wisley, East Malling Research Station (fruit), Long Ashton Research Station (fruit), National Vegetable Research Station, Glasshouse Crops Research Institute, etc.

In addition the RHS holds fortnightly shows at their headquarters in Vincent Square, London. Each autumn two of the shows are enlarged to allow space for fruit and vegetables. One of these special events held in September is known as the Great Autumn Show, followed by the Fruit and Vegetable Show in October, occasions when the leading amateur gardeners vie with each other for the premier awards. For the amateur fruit grower the shows provide a unique opportunity of seeing not only the best of a wide variety of fruit in the competitive classes but also an outstanding exhibit of fruit varieties grown and staged by the RHS, each variety is clearly labelled with its name, season of use, etc.

The extensive Wisley Gardens near Ripley in Surrey are open to Fellows (members of the RHS) free of charge, for non-members there is an entrance fee. Fruit and vegetable growing are strongly featured in the gardens, not only straightforward growing units but also in the well organized field trials. New and old varieties are submitted for field testing. Panels of expert judges visit the trials throughout the growing season, report and award when appropriate a certificate of merit.

Fellows of the RHS are also able to obtain help with their technical problems: the scientific staff based at the Wisley Laboratories deal with queries on subjects such as pests and diseases, weed control, specialized plant growing etc.

The library housed at the RHS headquarters in Vincent Square, London, is unique, both for its size and quality. Reference to it and the right to borrow books is available to Fellows of the RHS.

The Society publishes numerous books, including a monthly journal *The Garden* in which there is a regular feature 'The kitchen garden'. The journal is mailed each month free to all Fellows but is also available through booksellers at 65p per copy.

Applications for Fellowship should be addressed to:
The Secretary,
The Royal Horticultural Society,
Vincent Square,
London SW1P 2PE.

Individual fellowship costs £7.50 and two people can join for £12.00.

RESEARCH STATIONS

Government Research and Experimental Stations are concerned with work on commercial fruit and vegetable growing problems and are not normally able to provide assistance to the amateur gardener, but the general public are admitted on 'open days'. Educational exhibits together with demonstrations and lectures at such events enables the enquiring gardener to keep abreast with the latest development in horticultural technology and research.

Research stations: Fruit

East Malling Research Station (Agricultural Research Council) East Malling, nr. Maidstone, Kent.

Long Ashton Research Station (University of Bristol), Long Ashton, nr. Bristol.

Luddington Experimental Station (Ministry of Agriculture), Luddington, nr. Stratford-on-Avon, Warwickshire.

Vegetables

National Vegetable Research Station (Agricultural Research Council), Wellesbourne, nr. Warwick, Warwickshire.

Glasshouse crops

Glasshouse Crop Research Institute (Agricultural Research Institute), Rustington, nr. Littlehampton, Sussex.

COURSES

Many local authorities include horticulture in their adult education courses. Where available such courses do provide the student with the opportunity either to acquire more general horticultural knowledge or to delve more deeply into a particular facet of the subject. For information on adult horticultural education enquiries should be directed to the Education Department of the local authority.

Book list

The vast number of gardening books written on the subject of either fruit or vegetable growing make a bewildering display on the shelves of the average bookshop. This book written as an introduction to 'Growing your own food' can only whet the appetite and hope that the quest for still more knowledge will now go on. A wise move before deciding to buy a certain book is to borrow it from your local library, saving yourself not only disappointment but also money.

Further reading can be rewarding not only by increasing knowledge but by shortening the time between entering the realms of horticulture as a novice and the satisfying experience of growing your own fruit and vegetables successfully. The RHS has published two volumes, one on vegetable growing and one on fruit growing, both a must for the amateur gardener.

The Vegetable Garden Displayed
Royal Horticultural Society, 1975, £1.50.
This is a simple straight-forward guide to cultivation and methods of vegetable growing. Nearly 300 illustrations superbly presented in black and white, make it easy to follow the proceedings step-by-step. Crops included are those that can be grown outdoors in Britain such as beans, brassicas, rootcrops, onions and shallots, lettuces, tomatoes and also asparagus, artichokes both globe and Jerusalem, marrows, cucumbers and sweetcorn. Includes chapters on tools, digging, irrigation and machinery and a monthly calendar of vegetable gardening reminders. A valuable book both for the beginner and the experienced gardener alike.

The Fruit Garden Displayed
Royal Horticultural Society, 1975, £1.50.
This is the companion volume to **The Vegetable Garden Displayed,** and has a similar content of practical information and pictures all relating to the production of quality fruit in the garden. There are over 200 black and white photographs of excellent quality. The crops covered are strawberries, raspberries, black-, red and white currants, gooseberries, blackberries and various hybrid berries, apples, pears, plums, peaches, nectarines, cherries and figs. Subjects covered are planning the fruit garden, manuring, pruning, control of pests and diseases, propagation and the neglected fruit garden. A list of varieties recommended for garden cultivation is included. A book really up to date on the subject, particularly important at the present time as so many other publications available are now outdated as a result of rapid progress in pest and disease control, rootstock varieties, pruning, etc. A valuable book for all amateur fruit growers.

The Complete Book of Vegetables and Herbs
Roy Genders, Ward Lock, 1972, £4.50.
A book written by an expert in the art of vegetable growing, expensive but value for money. This book is divided in four parts. Part 1 deals with designing and planning the vegetable garden, greenhouses and coldframes, tools and equipment, soil preparation and drainage, propagation and planting, harvesting and storing. Part 2 is an ABC of vegetables, part 3 deals with the ever more popular herbs and their culture while part 4 tells the history of vegetables. A valuable book.

Simple Vegetable Growing
Roy Genders, Ward Lock, 1973, £1.25.
A very sound publication, full of information and written by an authority on the subject.

Dig This
Peter Seabrook, BBC, 1976, 40p.
A paperback of 62 pages packed solid with sound information on vegetable growing, well illustrated in colour and a reliable guide for the beginner and the seasoned gardener.

Vegetable Plotter
Dr. D. G. Hessayon, Pan Brittannica Industries Ltd, 1976, 40p.
A book in which each vegetable crop is allotted a separate page. Includes information on seeds, soil, sowing and planting, looking after crops, harvesting and varieties, together with expected harvesting or picking times. Line drawings and tables are freely used to illustrate the recommendations with pages devoted to basic rules, the vegetable plot cropping plan, spraying and watering, feeding and manuring.

For those interested in beating the record a page at the end of the book lists the UK record weights for every vegetable mentioned.

The Small Greenhouse
Deenagh Goold-Adams, The Royal Horticultural Society, 1974, 60p.
A complete guide to growing plants in a greenhouse. For the vegetable grower there are chapters on site and structure, heating and ventilation, watering and humidity, soils and feeding, plants from seed.

Growing Food for your Freezer
Jim Mather, W. Foulsham & Co. Ltd, 1975, £2.20.
A well presented book on fruit and vegetables with the emphasis on varieties more suitable for the freezer. The author stresses the need for crop planning to ensure maximum usable yields and claims that this can be achieved by picking both fruit and vegetables at the peak of their condition, some for immediate use and the remainder consigned without delay to the freezer. Rapid clearance of the ground allows space for a follow-on crop. The book deals thoroughly with freezing and thawing before ending on a horticultural note on pests and diseases and weeds.

Growing for the Show Bench
Brian Turner, Wolfe Publishing Ltd, 1973, 35p.
A series of small useful booklets: *Prizewinning Onions and Leeks, Prizewinning Potatoes, Prizewinning Tomatoes, Prizewinning Beans.* These booklets have been written for people with a common interest of growing for the show-bench rather than for the kitchen, although the point is made that exhibition vegetables are still good vegetables for the table. The exhibitor is concerned with uniformity, vegetables without a blemish and sometimes rather larger than the usual run of the garden grown specimens. Varieties most suitable for exhibiting are given, as are the cultural techniques. Very useful booklets for the would-be exhibitor and for the gardener simply interested in growing first-class vegetables.

The Practical Gardener's Encyclopedia
Compiled by Professor Alan Gemmell, Collins, 1977, £5.95.
Every aspect of gardening is fully discussed in this book by various very well known horticulturists, all experts in their own field. A full year's calendar is included. Deals with vegetables, fruit, flowers, shrubs, lawns, greenhouses, houseplants and has general tips for each month. An expensive book but worth the money because of the wide gardening subjects which it covers.

GARDENING PAPERS

Whilst most daily and weekly newspapers feature regular gardening articles contributed by gardening experts, the limited space available and the breadth of the subject does result in a little of everything without continuity on any particular section including fruit or vegetable growing. For up-to-date reading, week by week gardening papers such as *Amateur Gardening, Popular Gardening, Garden News,* etc. can be recommended.

Amateur Gardening
IPC Magazines Ltd, weekly at 15p.
It carries several regular articles on fruit and vegetable growing written to provide the reader with the fullest possible information, not only on the subject of growing but also full details about varieties to plant or sow for quality. Has articles on pest and disease control and many other features plus reminders about what needs to be done that week in the garden.

Popular Gardening
IPC Magazines Ltd, weekly at 15p.
Similar to Amateur Gardening in many respects but perhaps with less emphasis on growing vegetables and fruit. Has a first class gardening calendar.

Gardening News
EMAP National Publications Ltd, weekly at 15p in newspaper format.
This publication is meant as a gardening newspaper and carries news of what has been happening recently in the gardening world. Whilst reporting is its strong feature, regular articles are contributed on fruit and vegetable growing.

Practical Gardening
EMAP National Publications Ltd, monthly at 35p.
Has articles on fruit and vegetables written by regular well known contributors.

Whichever gardening paper is your choice, the best value and the maximum benefit will be derived from taking the same paper regularly. In all the papers fruit and vegetables are well covered with regular articles in series designed for continuity reading and the building up of the reader's horticultural knowledge.

Glossary

Acid: Applied to a soil deficient in lime as opposed to an alkaline or chalk soil. Serious acidity must be corrected by liming, but this should not be overdone. Check with a simple testing kit if in doubt.

Activator: Chemical or organic manure used to hasten decomposition of vegetable waste in compost heap or of straw in preparing mushroom bed.

Axil: Point where a leaf-stalk joins a stem and from which side-shoots arise, as in the tomato.

Berry: Fleshy fruit containing seeds.

Blanch: To deprive part of a plant of colouring matter by growing it in the dark, improving flavour quality. With celery this is done by earthing up, with chicory by growing in a dark place or under a light-tight cover.

Blind: non-flowering, due to some accident, disease, or deficiency.

Bolt: To run to seed before the crop is mature. May be due to climatic conditions, poor soil, lack of water or overcrowding. Leafy crops and root vegetables are those chiefly affected.

Bract: Modified leaves just below a flower. Often brightly coloured and resembling a flower, such as poinsettia.

Brassicas: Crops nearly related to the cabbage and including brussels sprouts, caulitlowers and calabrese. Swedes and turnips are allied to the brassicas and suffer equally from club root disease and the insect pest, flea beetle.

Broadcast: To sow seed by scattering it on the surface and raking it in or throwing soil over it. May be used for late sowings of root crops or of mustard for green manure.

Bulb: Underground storage organ derived from a bud.

Bulbil: Immature bulb, often budded off from mature bulb.

Calcifuge: A lime-hating plant, succeeding in acid soils. Few edible crops except the blueberry are true calcifuges but many prefer a very slightly acid soil.

Catch crop: One grown on vacant ground prepared for another crop. It must mature quickly and not delay the planting of the major crop. Thus lettuces on a site prepared for brussels sprouts may be interplanted with the latter if they have not been cleared.

Compost: Vegetable matter decomposed to the point at which it breaks down into plant nutrients in the soil. Also seed and potting composts: special soils for growing in containers, providing a maximum supply of plant foods.

Crown: The point from which stems spread from the roots, usually just above soil level.

Cultivar: Plant variety bred in cultivation.

Curd: The white edible head of the cauliflower.

Cutting: Section of plant used to grow a new plant.

Dormant: Not in active growth, literally 'sleeping'. Deciduous trees and bushes are transplanted when dormant so that roots can become established before the growing season.

Drill: Shallow trench in which seed is sown. A drill of even depth is necessary for small seeds and this requires a fine tilth and a level surface.

Earthing up: Drawing soil round a plant, to blanch the stems in the case of celery and to cover the tubers more deeply in the case of potatoes.

Emergence: Appearance of seedlings from the soil. Generally referred to as germination, though seeds may germinate well and yet fail to emerge owing to poor soil conditions.

Fertilizer: Chemical supplying one or more essential plant foods. Best regarded as only supplementing organic manures which also maintain the physical soil structure.

Frost hollow: Low ground where the coldest air collects in a radiation frost. To be avoided when planting early-flowering fruits.

Good heart: Vague term for soil inherently fertile or rendered so by consistently generous treatment, even though not recently manured or dressed with fertilizer.

Growing on: Used to describe treatment of seedlings under glass after pricking out. Important for young plants at this stage to have ample light and room for sturdy development.

Hardening-off: Gradual acclimatization of glass-raised plants to outdoor conditions by exposing them for gradually increasing periods. Vital before planting out tender crops such as tomatoes.

Hardy: A plant that overwinters or is started outdoors in spring while frost is still possible. Tender or half-hardy crops are sensitive to frost and bad weather generally. The description is not exact. Carrots are technically hardy but seedlings are affected by spring frosts. Sweetcorn is half-hardy but survives temperatures fatal to marrows.

Humus: The organic content of soil formed by the breakdown of animal and vegetable matter. Essential to fertility and soil structure.

Hybrid: Variety produced by crossing other varieties. An ordinary hybrid breeds true to type by self-fertilization. An F_1 hybrid is bred anew each season by the crossing of distinct parent lines.

Lateral: Side shoot or branch growing from a main branch or stem.

Leader or leading shoot: Tip of a branch or stem where growth and the extension of length takes place.

Legume or leguminous plant: A pod-bearer. Apart from their nutritional value as sources of protein, such plants are unique in their ability to gather atmospheric nitrogen through the bacteria in their root nodules.

Loam: Medium, fertile soil, rich in humus.

Midrib: Large central vein in a leaf.

Mulch: Material applied to the soil to reduce moisture loss by evaporation. May also have nutritive value and help to suppress weeds. Very important in culture of shallow-rooted soft fruit like raspberries and blackcurrants.

Open: Condition of soil through which water drains freely and which roots penetrate easily. Also, winter weather without hard frost or heavy rain, suitable for planting.

Organic gardening: Methods in which no inorganic fertilizers are used, only organic manures and compost, and the use of herbicides and pesticides is restricted.

Pan: A hard impervious upper layer of subsoil, which needs only to be broken up with a fork.

Pollination: Transference of pollen from the male to the female organs of the flower, whether of the same flower, another flower on the same plant, or flowers on different plants. The latter is often necessary to effect the fertilization of fruit blossom and for this flying insects are an essential carrying agent.

Pot bound: Condition in which a plant's root system is too large for the pot and the quantity of compost in which it is growing. Symptoms are rapid drying out after watering, stunted and yellowing growth, roots appearing on the surface of the compost and enclosing the soil ball in a dense network. Repot or plant out promptly. It is important not to start too early when raising tender crops under glass for outdoor planting, as they may suffer in this way before it is safe to plant.

Prostrate: Of low, spreading habit, like the trailing marrow. Prostrate plants occupy more space in relation to yield than upright or climbing ones.

Ring culture: Method of greenhouse tomato growing. So called because the containers are bottomless cylinders of compost standing on a layer of some water-holding but sterile medium. Useful where plants cannot be watered frequently.

Runner: Creeping stem bearing one or more plantlets, which take root and are detached from the parent as separate plants.

Seed: Product of fertilization from which a new plant will grow.

Seed-leaf: Seed-leaves or cotyledons are the first to appear on germination and are usually different in form to the true leaves. If destroyed or badly damaged, the seedling dies, so it is important to protect them from insects such as flea beetle.

Set: A fruit successfully fertilized and beginning to swell is said to have set. When a large percentage of flowers produce developing fruit it is referred to as 'a good set'.

Soft fruit: Fruit produced on bushes, canes or plants, as distinct from *top fruit*, produced on trees. The term is not always descriptive; a green gooseberry is technically a soft fruit though in fact very hard.

Soil mulch: Layer of loose soil produced by regular surface cultivation, obstructing passage of moisture to the surface and reducing evaporation loss.

Spit: Depth of soil penetrated by fork or spade inserted to full length of tines or blade. Often nearly coincides with depth of topsoil.

Spur: Short twiggy growth. A fruiting spur bears fruit buds in which are the embryo blossoms. Much pruning aims at encouraging the development of fruiting spurs.

Stop: To pinch out the growing point at the tip of a leading shoot. The usual effect is to encourage the development of laterals and generally bushy growth, as in the dwarfing of runner beans.

Successional cropping: This has two rather different meanings. Successional small sowings are made of a crop such as lettuces to ensure continuity of supply and minimum wastage, or one crop is cleared away on completion and followed by a different one for harvesting in the same season, as when a quick-maturing crop follows early potatoes.

Sucker: A new growth from a root or the base of a stem. Suckers are sometimes a nuisance, as when they spring up round the leg of a gooseberry or from the rootstock of a fruit tree, and they must then be removed. In the case of raspberries and globe artichokes they are the normal means of propagation.

Tilth: Literally, soil that has been tilled. In practice, the topmost layer of soil in a fine, crumbly condition for sowing. A tilth obtained by mechanical means such as raking is said to be 'forced' and is not as good as that obtained by exposure to frost and other forms of weathering.

Top dressing: Application of fertilizer or fresh compost to the soil surface.

Truss: Several flowers or fruits carried on one stem, as in the tomato and strawberry.

Tuber: Root acting as food store resembling bulb or rhizome.

Variety: A named form of a species. Varieties of the garden pea, for instance, differ greatly in habit and other characteristics important to the gardener, but botanically they are the same. Varieties are ultimately derived from wild species by selection, cross-breeding and the occurrence of mutations or sports. The word *cultivar* also means a named cultivated variety.

Waterlogging: Retention of surplus water in the soil owing to bad drainage. Saturation results in air being excluded from between soil particles and roots and soil bacteria suffering from lack of oxygen. Pipe drainage is sometimes necessary, but often the trouble is due to *pan*.

Index

Numbers in italics indicate illustrations.

Credits

Artists
Jon Blake
Pamela Dowson
Ron Hayward Art Group
Vanessa Luff
Ralph Stobart

Photographs
Alfieri: 49
Fisons: 7
Clay Perry: 5, 21, 29, 40, 72
Harry Smith: 73, 77, 81
Suttons Seeds: 52/3

Cover
Design: Barry Kemp
Photograph: Paul Forrester